EDITOR: NADER TEHRANI

BOOK DESIGNER / EDITOR: NICOLE SAKR

DRAWINGS: HARRY LOWD, LISA LACHARITÉ, GARY LIN

TRANSCRIPTION: NATHAN VICE, TOFAN RAFATI, NICOLE SAKR

PHOTOGRAPHY: JOHN HORNER

THE ARBITRARY *IS* ARCHITECTURE

ROBERT LEVIT

Villa Varoise by NADAAA represents something of a departure from earlier dedications in Nader Tehrani's work. First as a founder of Office dA, and more recently of NADAAA, a defining characteristic of Tehrani's work has been concerned with what he has described as the relationship between figuration and configuration. He is referring to the correlation between the modularity of parts, of building parts and their patterning effects, and overall building form: bricks, blocks, panels, windows, and solar fins on the one hand; and building shape on the other. His own dedication to this issue pre-dated by at least a decade the centrality such issues acquired as the free-form surface experiments of architecture's early digital age became entangled in questions of actual building. (These entanglements led to a generation's interest in tessellation or the discretization of curved surfaces into building components and thus patterns.) In Tehrani's work, the modularity of elements—the configurations of tectonic assembly—was core from very early on in such projects as Casa la Roca, the Weston House, and the Toledo Residence, or even later in the Tongxian Gate House, the Macallen Building, and the recent Daniels Faculty of Architecture Building. In the now demolished BanQ restaurant interior, where smooth form was implied, the effect was obtained through discrete panels—which is to say, through modular patterning.

1.1

1.2

Villa Varoise's exterior walls are board-formed concrete. While true that through the imprint of this classic means of concrete forming the trace of modularity is imprinted on concrete's hardened liquid form, compared to the pronounced patterns of modular assembly dominant elsewhere in Tehrani's oeuvre, this project stands out. Its difference lies in the unifying plastic effects of poured-in-place concrete. It is this plastic formal quality—a body without parts—of this project that reveals characteristics of Tehrani's work that are otherwise and elsewhere less evident in Tehrani's projects. Villa Varoise's simpler concrete form reveals more nakedly the manipulations of type and geometry that are often otherwise subsumed in the exchange between complex modular behavior and building figure.

This book on the Villa Varoise is occasioned by a discussion that Tehrani conducted with his long- time colleague and friend, Preston Scott Cohen. In conversation with Cohen, Tehrani hoped to bring out ways in which this house, in particular, was an instance in which his work and Cohen's drew together; but also in ways they otherwise do not, or, if they do elsewhere, less evidently so. I imagine that for comparison's sake, the house by Cohen that Tehrani had in mind was one of long ago: the Torus house. This house belonged to a period of work by Cohen done in the 1990s, when most of his projects remained unbuilt and were rendered in immaterial and highly plastic form—in architect's white.

The Torus house was a raised courtyard house (somewhat like the Villa Varoise) that was disturbed, so to speak, by a line or contour that moved through it; or as if by a cord being drawn through the fabric of the house, twisting its elemental square courtyard form and giving rise to something akin to a standing wave's crest in its surfaces. Now, while subtle distortions of form have been a part of Tehrani's work since early on, they have always seemed to arise from the manipulation of modular arrays in elastic patterns of brick—transforming into screens, corbelling over in subtle curves, and otherwise patterned (Tongxian); or in arborial bracketed columns appearing in forest-like variety (Issam Fares Institute); or in the many projects that deal with panel-patterned façades; or spatial cellular arrays (Modernas Meno Centras, the Daniels Building, and the Melbourne School of Design).

1.3

Pattern does not disappear entirely from Villa Varoise. But, neither the subtle fact of the board-formed concrete, nor the series of thin cast-concrete posts screening the bedrooms acquire that degree of articulation or reciprocity between patterning element and building form found elsewhere in Tehrani's work. Over the main living spaces, folding ceiling forms hover, rising into the creased roof of the entry façade and subsiding into the straight and level horizontal of the living room's courtyard elevation. But, while these creased forms resemble the variable spatial-structural modules in other projects, here the folding is of a more continuous form—absorbed into the continuities of surfaces and volumes of the whole house.

What is striking about this house is the degree to which it is free of that defining tectonic of combinatory patterns otherwise so characteristic in Tehrani's work. The consequence is to reveal more nakedly Tehrani's interest in the plastic modeling of form on the one hand, and the related interest in the mutation of typological figures on the other.

The diagrams that accompany the presentation of the Villa Varoise design show a simple rectangular courtyard figure that is transformed by breaking it into upper and lower L-forms, allowing the house to step down the sloped site. The courtyard, now partially exposed, must resolve its relationship to the diagonal created by these two bracketing L's. In the diagrams the courtyard is simply divided along its diagonal. In the finished design this diagonal develops sectionally: a portion of one of the courtyard's triangular halves slopes down—a descending landscape upon which stairs are placed. (The other triangular half of the courtyard is made into a pool, the boundaries of which maintain the visible imprint of the courtyard figure on a terrace extended over the lower wing of the house.) This topographical modeling of the courtyard produces the most dramatic corner of the house where it cantilevers out over the site and the ground rises up through the building. The sculptural configuration of the house at this corner captures in plastic form the dynamic reconfiguration of the basic courtyard type that has recast the form of the house: its stepped L-forms, the resultant diagonals, and the distorted corner angles (the original rectangular figure of the house diagram has been transformed into a parallelogram,

VV

conforming more precisely to the fall of the site, and accentuating the diagonal of the courtyard).

Tehrani has for many years accompanied his projects with diagrams similar to those of this project, which is to say that the transformations of elemental shapes and types is not new to this project. It is simply that the material nature of this house—the monolithic and plastic qualities of poured-in-place concrete—brings out qualities that otherwise only shadow the more evident dynamics of pattern and tectonic assembly prevailing elsewhere in Tehrani's work.

The elemental form of the Villa Varoise, derived from its material simplicity and the consequently more visible formal manipulations of type—its mannered distortions of form—draws this particular project by Tehrani into closer orbit to the characteristic idiom and formal explorations in Cohen's work. Otherwise, the trajectories of their two respective bodies of work have followed, in consequential ways, separate paths. This book is an occasion to think about what is at stake in the difference between two architects who emerged from a shared milieu and what project for architecture might still be shared between them.

Tehrani stood out amongst student-days peers that included Cohen. What was startling from early on in Tehrani's work was its dedication since those early years, in the mid-1980s, to a tectonic vocation. While there were a handful of classmates who shared something of his interest, the prevailing idiom of the time, whether it drew upon the waning post-modern historicist influences or a returning taste for the neo-modern, was generally speaking materially and formally abstract—abstract in the sense of combining the formal elementalism of modernist architectural work (of an early Corbusian flavor) with a more contemporary orientation to immateriality unconcerned with construction or material substance.

1.4

In those days Tehrani was interested in a variety of architects and architectures—from the tectonic patterning of the Seljuk and Safavid periods to the form-finding experiments found in modular inventions undertaken by architects such as Miguel Fisac and Eladio Dieste. What interested him in these various bodies of work was the interplay between patterning elements and building form. These interests stood out against the backdrop of the more prevalent taste focused on the combination of elemental forms, formal syntactical operations, and immaterial abstraction prevailing in architecture schools of the American Northeast.

Whence this taste then (and returning) for material abstraction? What has and continues to subtend the commitments of immaterial forms of abstraction? I realize that what I am about to write relies upon a number of clichés. But, I believe that they are clichés that were and continue to be formative of architectural tastes and practices. Works that fall into the category of abstract formalism are deemed timeless—free of tastes, good or bad, that attach to architectures identified, negatively, with styles. Yes, this view means subscribing to the untenable notion that abstract formalism is not itself a particular episode of taste formation. But, regardless, tacit assumptions that a certain abstract style transcends questions of style endure. When many decades ago Meyer Schapiro observed that sensibilities forged in the appreciation of abstract form were sensibilities made ready for appreciating works from any historical period or place—independent of a work's original purpose or significance—the unintended and erroneous corollary was that abstract forms are timeless. His observation pointed to a tempting if fallacious idea about abstract form.

Schapiro's observation of a half-century ago has now gained new traction linked to digital media, in general, and social media, in particular. The seeming immaterial flow of images complemented in designers' experiences of digital design tools renders all experience as if it were immaterial and in that sense abstract. The world as information, as immaterial pattern, is a seductive aspect of digitally shaped experience, regardless of whether it belies the ongoing and durably incarnate fact of human beings and the material world they inhabit—and through which the digital world flows.

In contrast to such notions of the abstract and the immaterial, things made through the contingencies of craft and visible assembly draw attention to the embodied here and now. They provide evidence of their making and of the transience of their substance.

While abstraction makes erroneous if seductive claims to being suprastylistic, patterning, particularly of surfaces, but more generally of elements is rife with so many options that the question of ornament and its arbitrary and taste-driven judgments present themselves. (Here I am drawing into a single circle ornament, taste, and style.) True, the pattern of building assemblies and of tectonic systems, more often than not are treated as and judged as if they were the indices of building facts, and if not exactly straightforward facts, then as guarantors of quality and legitimacy founded upon the material ontology of a building. But, whether this notion of index (of indexicality) is ever sufficient explanation of the myriad judgments rendered in any building design, and whether a putative ontology of materials does anything but obfuscate the real symbolic discourse shaping buildings, notions such as index do not at all capture what is at stake in Tehrani's work.

In his work, there is a reciprocity between the elastic nature of patterns and the manipulations of underlying plastic aspects of a building form. Patterned elements stretch and contract, and are otherwise permuted to accommodate underlying forms. Yet this reciprocity between elements and figures, or again as Tehrani himself puts it, between configuration and figuration, is a machine of sorts for the production of ornament. Thus, while the interaction between, let us say, brick and curvature, index the relationship of shape and module, the confluence of mannered forms conjoined with unusual patternings tilt towards the arbitrary and customary qualities of ornament and away from didactic clarity or tectonic transparency. Though Tehrani does not use the word ornament in his

1.6

essay with his former partner Monica Ponce de Leon, "Versioning: Connubial Reciprocity of Surface and Space", the article does elaborate ambitions derived from the imbricated systems of modular assemblies and form. They are clear that the systems of assembly and how they are caught up in determining bigger and subtler formal possibilities are not "architectural facts" but "arbitrary" choices. Rather than ornament, they preferred the words "semantic and experiential effect." To my mind ornament captures more directly the central importance of an arbitrary choice (or "arbitrary reason" as Tehrani originally put it) in the elaboration of effects made through the "connubial" confluence of modularity and shapely form.

What is clear in Tehrani's work is the commitment to fashioning an inseparable bond between pattern and forms made through the marriage between systems of assembly and the spatial, typological, and otherwise manipulated forms of a building. The term ornament, if it falls short of capturing this deep imbrication of systems, is nevertheless useful in pointing more explicitly towards the arbitrary nature of the effects that result: these results are neither indexes of necessity, nor truth in materials. And while it may seem that Tehrani's works subscribe to a notion of the organic body made through the union of matter and form, arbitrary choices, formal a prioris tangle together in his work. As I have argued elsewhere (in "Contemporary Ornament, Return of the Symbolic Repressed") ornament, rather than bearing the marks of construction or craft, is more properly understood as the arbitrary maintenance of unnecessary markings, patterns, and elements disconnected from whatever origins that might once have given rise to their forms. Tehrani tempts us to see his works as bearers of some truth about the nature of materials while revealing the impulse toward arbitrary and ornamental effect which is in fact, amongst other things, a liberation from the truth of materials. An examination and comparison of Tehrani's work to that of an architect he admired, Eladio Dieste, can be illustrative. Recently, Tehrani traveled to Uruguay to see the work of Eladio Dieste, one of the key figures whom he has admired since his student-days. Dieste's work was unique amongst such early and middle twentieth-century engineer/architects as Felix Candela, Eduardo Torroja, and the somewhat earlier Robert Maillart. These architects, all developing thin-shell forms, did so in concrete, with the exception of Dieste, who developed a composite system of brick and concrete, lending to his work a modularity of surface distinct from his peers and appreciated in detail by Tehrani in his recent article "Probable Architectures of Improbable Reason, Confluence in the Work of Eladio Dieste: A Belated Book Review." But, lest his affection for the Uruguayan architect place him too closely in league with Dieste's particular vocation, an important distinction needs making. The larger ordering forms of Dieste's buildings, resonant though they were with familiar historical types, were certainly made strange by the performative geometries of thin-shell construction. Nevertheless, the confluence in Dieste's work of historical forms and new shaping geometries ultimately resulted in regular, figural, and structural types free of the intricacies and distortions that consistently appear in Tehrani's work. These intricacies and distortions of

1.7

figure in Tehrani's work, complicit as they almost always are with the complications of modular systems, give rise to the characteristic confluence of ornamental effect and assembly systems that runs throughout his body of work.

1.8

Let us return then to comparisons between Cohen's and Tehrani's work. What they share is perhaps more evident in the comparison of this later work by Tehrani, Villa Varoise, and Cohen's early Torus House. Villa Varoise, more stripped than usual of the modular syntax typical of Tehrani, and coincidentally similar to the Torus house by virtue of their shared courtyard forms, invites the comparison. In what seems like a special case, we can see a shared interest in the way typological forms in their respective bodies of work suffer distortions—mannered treatments that twist and rack a building's primary forms and develop consequences in countless details, which themselves are as much the point as the larger scale modifications of type.

But what of these two architects' differences? Tehrani and Cohen were both educated in the same northeast corridor milieu of the 1980s at RISD and the GSD and are heirs to its architectural culture. They were influenced by the combined interests in historical type and the intricacies of formal syntax. The propagation of the first, the focus on type, revolved around the influence in the US of Aldo Rossi, but also of many other related figures including Rodolfo Machado and Jorge Silvetti, and a myriad of European rationalists new and old; while the involutions of distortion or of formal "transformation" were linked to the influence of Peter Eisenman, Robert Venturi and many other figures.

1.9

But again, what of the difference? The abstraction of form and the immaterial formalism of Cohen adhered to characteristics of a seminal phase of Modernist architecture, distilled in the whiteness of the Weissenhof housing project, but married to what was in the 1980s the contemporary predilection for an architecture of pure formal intellection. At Weissenhof and in the early work of Le Corbusier, and many other white moderns, attributes of a new industrial architecture were secondary to an aesthetic project of "timeless" geometries, resonant, as many have observed, with the whiteness of Mediterranean vernacular forms and whitewashed notions of antiquity, but, in either case, oriented towards an idea of timelessness opposed to the "misuse" of historical styles. Aside from the ongoing appeal, explicitly or simply tacitly inherited from Le Corbusier's notions of architecture as the "plastic play of form in light," we might add that within elite schools of architecture, the distance from building would appeal to both professors and students whose experience and identity enjoyed its remoteness from material, from trades, and craft—a distance articulated in the very foundations of the architectural discipline.

1.10

Yet, Tehrani's work was never this "white" architecture. (In fact, Tehrani's thesis at RISD addressed the later concrete phase of Le Corbusier's work and in particular the Unité d'habitation, its concrete formwork, and the role of construction in recasting Le Corbusier's ideas.) And, while Villa Varoise foregoes many of the characteristic modes of expression found elsewhere in his oeuvre, it's not as if its board-formed concrete (and the clarity with which it foregrounds more plastic attributes of the house) is somehow immaterial. Also, it's not as if Tehrani's early and persistent interests in tectonic systems put him into some sort of *Baukunst* camp, narrowly focused on the material art of building. The imbrication of pattern-making materials and form, configuration and figuration, was no less an act of formalist intellection than that of peers like Cohen. However, the vocation he chose in exploring the modular behavior of materials, of systems, has meant his architecture has inclined towards the fabricated artifact. The interactions between modular elements, variably sized, or shaped, or positioned, even where the elements are of the utmost contemporary and manufactured sort, summon an idea of making, of being made, or at least of trades and the procedures of assembly. However, one might put it, the materiality of his buildings is more present, more a protagonist in his work. Perhaps in some of the bigger buildings of his more recent work, paneled enclosure systems belong to more familiar and ubiquitous building strategies, but his ongoing attempt to subtly manipulate patterns, to do so in ways that are bound up with the plastic behavior of his buildings, seeks to re-establish the interaction between the artful flexibility of crafting buildings with more contemporary and abstract systems, and impersonal modes of labor.

1.11

Yet, as different as Tehrani's and Cohen's respective works have been, perhaps the immaterial whiteness of Cohen's earlier work (and a way of developing form that persists today even after his having come to terms with its material incarnations) and Tehrani's commitment to an order of assembly, are differences that belie shared commitments. The formal and aesthetic principles in both architects' work—the manipulation of type, the mannered twists of form obvious in Cohen's work and more camouflaged in Tehrani's work, and the complexities of pattern in Tehrani's work—all reflect métiers shaped not by the discovery nor revelation of what is necessary, but by architecture's liberation from necessity.

The works are not distillations of what is essential to architecture, nor demonstrations of how contingency (of actual buildings, programs and sites) shuffles the specifics of type, nor exposés of systems of assembly. Rather, these works share in showing what is arbitrary, which is to say, what makes architecture an art that is not a metabolic satisfaction of need nor reflection of any number of putative necessities. The arbitrary is not a term of contempt but rather a recognition of that which distinguishes architecture from a heightened version of metabolic processes. Such architecture's virtue does not lie in learning from nature and emulating animals—their hives, dams, or nests—nor learning from organic or inorganic structures to produce an efficient logic of sheltering. It is the arbitrary that is the basis of the anthropogenesis that positions architecture against nature. Architecture is not a mimesis of some given world of things and life, such principals, patterns, structures or organizational logics (regardless of such claims where they may arise), but their transformation into a symbolic human habitat. Thus, if I may conflate the ornamental and symbolic purposes of architecture to make a point, it is the transformation of metabolic needs and the hideous flux of phenomenon into meaningful and arbitrary structures that make architecture itself and us, us. Ornament is shaping the necessary or the given into the meaningful. Thus, in Tehrani's work it is the ornamental result of patterns and formal manipulations, none of which are necessary, that is the defining mark of his work, rather than the discovery of a reconciliation with systems and forms.

Two final post-scripts:

First, against the backdrop of the new social-media-driven chapter unfolding around the role of representation through drawings—the questions of representation for these two architects reside entirely in the architectural object and neither has ever treated drawing as anything more than the description of that artifact.

Second, the material incarnation of pattern is now experienced at a moment when we have become habituated to the flexible modifications made possible through digital systems of design and customization. Cognition, recast by the experience of the world as digital information, is most developed amongst design professionals accustomed to the use of parametric software, but such cognitive habits are quite familiar in anyone's everyday experiences of simple text programs, or through entertainments such as *The Matrix*, or the TV series *Altered Carbon*, or countless related representations of the world as a malleable code and pattern. The incarnate patterns in Tehrani's buildings reside in an imaginary destabilized by the experience of the world as malleable code, yet what his buildings do is instantiate that illusory sense of immateriality in the ineluctable materiality of our incarnate habitat.

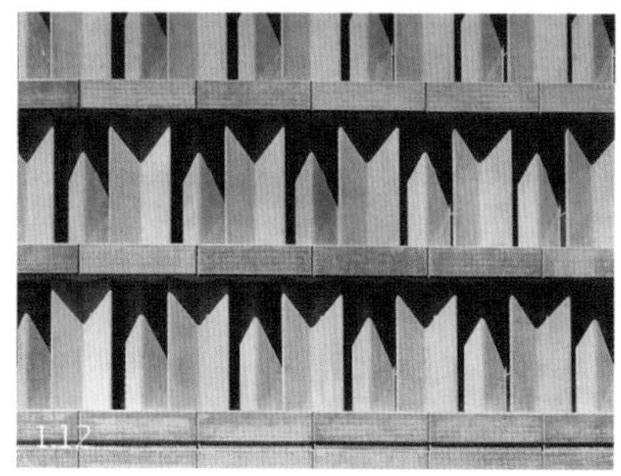

1.13

PROLOGUE: A USER'S MANUAL

NADER TEHRANI

This book is inspired by a discursive thirst, seeking to place the architectural act as part of a larger conversation with history and the architects who motivate those discussions. Villa Varoise emerges from a fascination with many histories, but in the context of this specific house, also the pedagogies of Preston Scott Cohen with whom I have had the luxury of conversations for over three decades; the house folds these narratives not only into its design, but also into the debates it produces. One could say that the conversation of this book preceded us and we enacted another chapter to extend it, hoping that others might take it forward from here. For this reason, the book is also formatted in such a way to allow that conversation to have three tenses in its layout.

Allowing the content of the book to read on its own terms, this prologue is merely a user's manual to better explain its graphic layout and the way in which the dialogue is framed. The book is structured around a conversation between Preston Scott Cohen and me, always laid out in the central column of the left side of each spread—printed in black text. The text is an edited transcription of an event held at the Harvard Graduate School of Design on April 16, 2012, entitled "*My House is Better Than Your House*." The editing evacuates some of the marginal detritus out of the text, while also making clarifications when the audio recording failed; however, the main arguments remain intact. To the left and right of this central text, there are added columns within which we have placed both images and texts: in the left margin, those used by Preston Scott Cohen, and in the right, those used by me. The images are drawn from the lecture, from references used within the talk, or from conversations afterwards. The text within the marginalia adds commentary to the original conversation with clarifications, changes of opinions, as well as new prompts. We have reserved the space on the right side of each spread for drawings, diagrams, construction photographs, and final images of Villa Varoise. The presentation of the house unfolds in accordance to the transcript, dispensing with the conventional linear explanation of a project—what is most often an alibi, a defense, or a fiction; instead, we allow the debate to reveal the project as part of its own meander. It is important to note that Preston Scott Cohen and I present each other's projects, not our own. Thus, as authors, we abdicate the primary interpretations of the houses, allowing the critic's voice to emerge and give a prominent light to the respective projects. Finally, with a debt of gratitude to Cohen, while the invitation to share a platform at Harvard was completely symmetrical, this book displays an asymmetry in that it focuses on Villa Varoise, using its completion as the opportunity to expose the discussion behind it. This book is also dedicated to a more in-depth architectural analysis of Villa Varoise: its drawings, diagrams, contract documents, and construction details, all of which attempt to give our debate a formal, spatial, and material dimension.

VILLA VAROISE

FAHMY HOUSE

APRIL 16, 2012

NADER TEHRANI AND PRESTON SCOTT COHEN

MY HOUSE IS BETTER THAN YOUR HOUSE

HARVARD UNIVERSITY GRADUATE SCHOOL OF DESIGN

PSC: Thank you for coming. This is really meant to be a rather casual discussion. That's why we held it as a lunch break. Basically, this is an event that was inspired by a conversation that's quite consistent with many that I have had with

FH

Nader. He called me up one day and he said, "In the past, I have had houses that I've wanted to share. For example, in my early career, I had a house for Rodolfo Machado and now, I have one for you". He told me to look at it, and when I did, I was quite surprised to see that indeed it was quite similar to a house that I had worked on for a long time, the Fahmy House in Los Gatos, California.

NT: In fact, it was a house I designed for Scott, in response to Scott's pedagogy, and investments, much like the Mill Road House that I had designed for Rodolfo. As such, it is at once a rebuttal, as much as it is a dedication.

2.1

His was so much more beautiful than mine and yet, the thought crossed my mind that I still believed my house was better. At that point, this was a new house from Nader that I had never seen, but mine had been around for far too long, since 2007. The story of why the Fahmy House had been dragging on for so long, but now would finally be built, is really kind of absurd, but of no particular interest. Anyway, I asked Nader to recollect for me the first time he had seen the Fahmy House because, as I recalled, at that time he had bitterly complained about many aspects of it. It seemed to me that he really did not like it. He later looked at newer renderings that represent the final design and said they were gross. He said they were in bad taste. He said there was a real taste problem. He really thought that the house had gone from bad to worse. I didn't see this invasion of bad taste in the project itself. And, as far as I was concerned, it was as beautiful or ugly as it was before. I thought it was more interesting than the houses that Nader had previously done. This new house by him, though, was the most restrained of any that I'd seen of his. This is what I preferred about it. It seemed more minimal and therefore to look, or even to be, more like my work. I liked it! So, it seemed this opened up something new. As his work was moving toward mine, I was liking it more and as my work was moving, I don't know where, he thought it was getting worse.

Nader and I share many interests; we really have been in the trenches for many years. He's one of the few people I can be honest with and he is honest with me. We have a rare relationship; he will tell me exactly what is wrong with what I am doing, and I will tell him what I think is wrong with what he's doing. It is a true, passionate sort of exchange and he was the inspiration for the GSD series called "Discussions in Architecture." To my mind, the first unofficial installment of the series was a discussion with him about his work at MIT.

2.2

Today will be different from those discussions. It will be bilateral, instead of one directional, because I'm implicated in this. I was a little bit uneasy about this idea, though, and almost switched back to the discussions format. I had

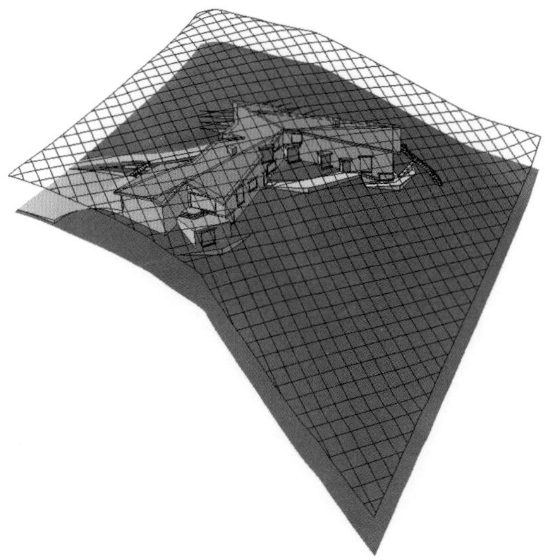

Fahmy House

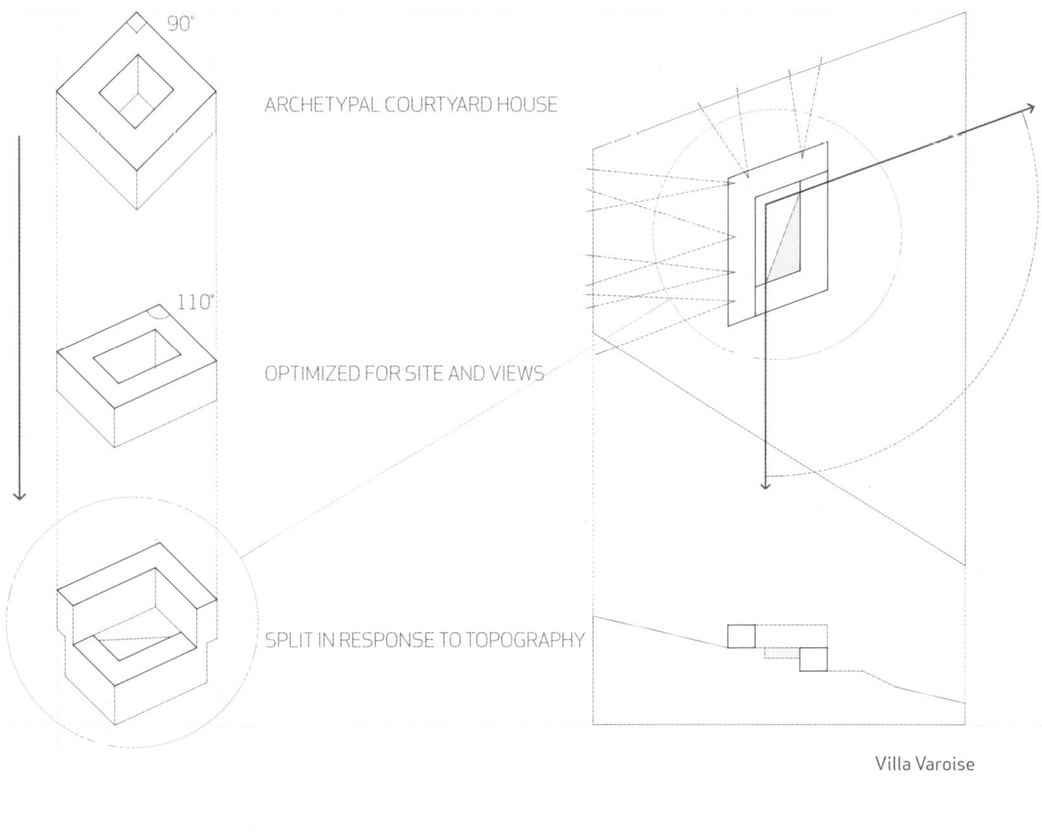

Villa Varoise

too much to say about Nader and I really didn't want to have him turn any of it back on me. This could potentially put me at a disadvantage. Anyway, I went ahead and decided it could be fun. It's time for us to openly out some of our disputes, in all their minutia. Ultimately, many of our differences are quite small. You could say we have the same background in many respects with parallel educations and we have both been teaching for years. Some would say our differences are absolutely of no consequence, but I believe that they really do exponentially open up interesting issues because we can actually get into things deeply rather than surfing over everything very horizontally.

I thought that Nader should begin because he will set the tone as the guest. Here is the format: he will make a presentation, very brief, as will I. We will both talk five or ten minutes. He'll do a brief presentation about my house, then I will present his. Each of us will speak about the other with reference to other general issues and each of us will respond to the other in a free and open dialogue. After that, the conversation will be widened to include you, the audience.

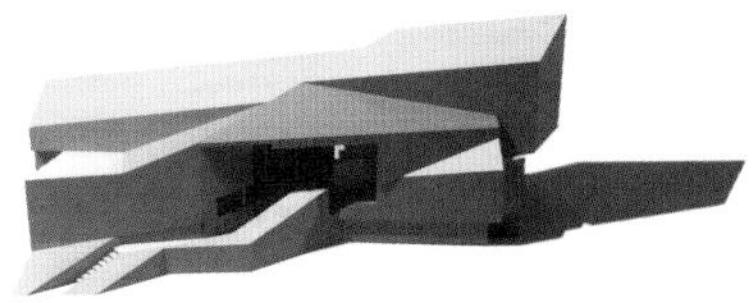

2.3

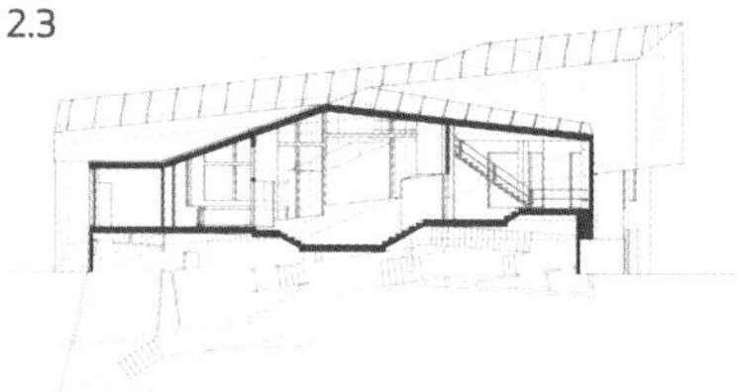

2.4
Cornered House, Preston Scott Cohen

NT: To complete the introduction, I would say that it's correct that my house is very much dedicated to Scott, but I wasn't actually thinking of the Fahmy house when I said "I have one for you". I was thinking about the trajectory of your work, more evident in the Torus House and the Wu House which are reflections on geometry's confrontation with typology; thus, my concerns revolve around a different set of issues than the obvious similarities between the Fahmy House and Villa Varoise, which are also legitimate. This is why we're going to talk about them today.

NT: I would also add the category of landscape to this, as the Torus House implicates the terrain in which it sits in a critical way.

In fact, you're absolutely right. I thought your house was ugly I didn't even consider it as something I would address, and now you've forced me to address it, but I'm more interested to talk about its typological problems, rather than delve into issues of taste or aesthetics. Some other anecdotes may come along the way, but we're going to present each other's work, so I'll try to be quick about things you've already presented yourself.

FH

In the Fahmy House there was an idea that because of the topography of the house, it could not be placed just anywhere. The connection to the road is so critical that there's only one place that the cars can come in, but the relationship with the trees is also important: you can't cut down the trees. This is why not only do the views privilege the downhill, but the bending of the form—the folding of the plan—responds to the location of the existing trees. The depression of

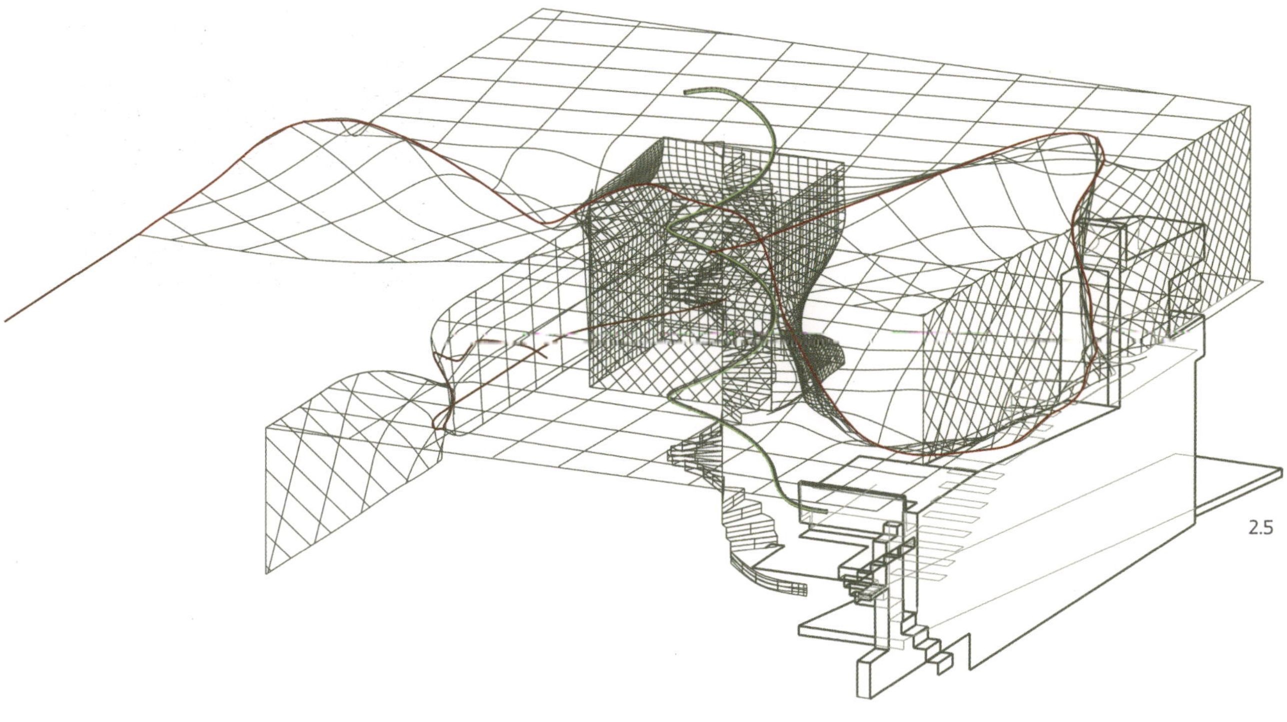

2.5

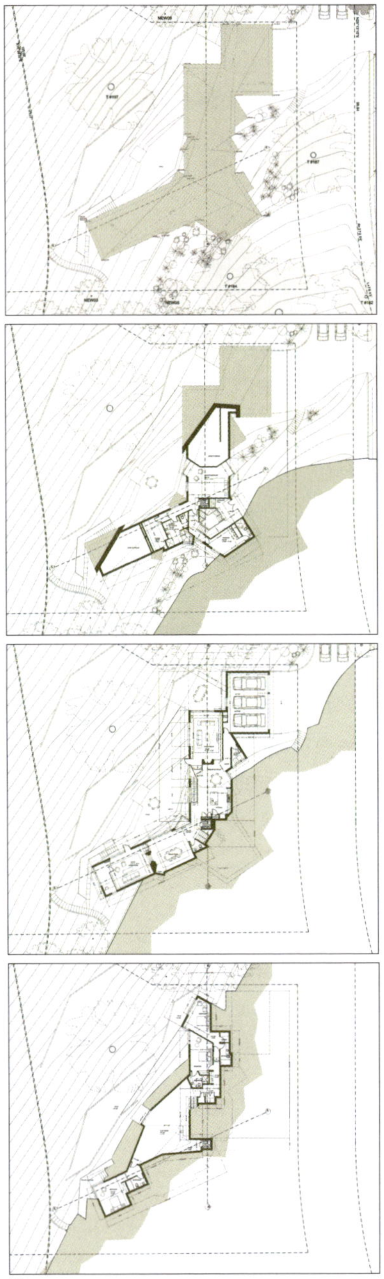

the house is actually the result of a zoning limitation which is almost identical to the limitations of the Villa Varoise site.

PSC: Yours…

NT: Yes, mine also. The zoning circumstances for the Fahmy House produce an "offset blanket," if you will: I love your image of this offset plane, because it's proto-architectural. It's almost the same way that you dealt with the Torus House model, the one you built for MoMA, where you objectified the landscape and all of the sudden it wasn't the base for the model alone, but it had its own iconic status. I like this challenge to the architectural convention. In the Fahmy House, when you finally materialize it—it becomes a more banal version of it, with its gestures towards site circumstances. It loses the power of the deformed plane. In fairness, the selection of materials does reinforce the suspended plane, because the roof is objectified, in separation from the volume of the house. In doing so, it establishes a rapport with a certain kind of history without radicalizing the very things that Wright did, in this case the plane being the kind of materialization of its relationship to the landscape. I'm not insisting that his is the only way to do it, but invariably your house establishes that dialogue.

NT: It did not naturalize the ground as many conventional models might, but by delaminating the ground, it brought attention to the landscape as a protagonist in the architectural conversation.

Kentucky Knob House, Frank Lloyd Wright

The site entry engages the parking level, which is at a lower level than the entry. The roof geometry is significant because it coalesces certain aspects of the "offset plane" of the site, which is important to its form. The drop-off draws you up the stairs to the main entry, after which you are immediately plummeted back down into the public level of the house. Thus, you bypass the master suite level entirely, and are enveloped by the figure of the entry lobby; the entry stair directs down one level on axis with the main view out towards the landscape...the payback of the entry sequence. The public level is characterized by a series of semi-open programs: in sequence, the family room, kitchen dining, and living room are situated in sequence in an open enfilade, wrapped around the landscape like a boomerang, looking towards the same panorama. It is important to note that other ramps organize the edge of the house, opening up the views but also giving access to the landscape, and a deck.

There's this curious thing where there's yet another floor of bedrooms and the stair comes down to another playroom; apparently landlocked, the whole room is in fact underneath the landscape berm. In discussions with Scott, I came to understand the importance of the geometry of this house, not only its roof and its

FH

plan, but also the landscape. There is a notion that the geometry of that berm could not be violated such that even areas like this retaining wall could not be shifted because of the insistence of a diagonal line that maintains a fidelity to a legible geometry within its court. In other projects Scott will objectify the line of the landscape, but so too, he will erase any evidence of the conventionality of retaining walls and the detritus of everyday life... not so in this project.

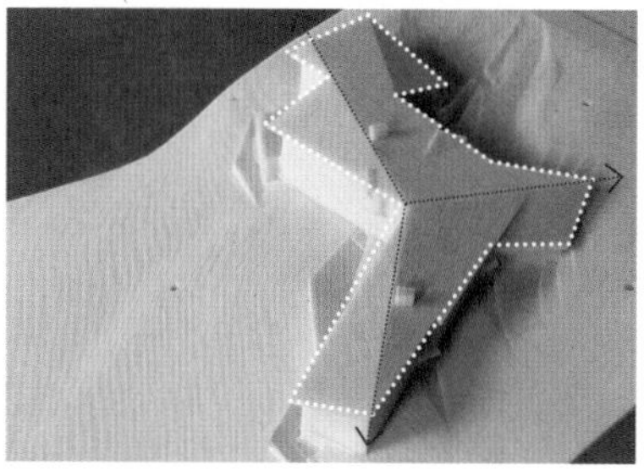

The roof has an insistent geometry. I can't say I understand it or know it well enough, but I understand its connection to other projects, the Goldman Sachs arcade project being one of them, which had an eccentric geometry which is held together with one single line that crosses the entire length of the arcade. So too, this house has a key set of geometries that operate on the ridges, basically giving you a hip roof, but triangulated coming down in all directions. But what's interesting actually is that you get into other geometric predicaments where a ridge on the center of a geometry all of a sudden hits an edge condition which means that the purity of that line is violated by virtue of the contingencies of drainage, tectonics of roof materials, and all of those things which you found ways of erasing in other projects. In other words, the coping, the gutter, and the stuff of conventional architecture is eradicated in other projects, so the question is how come you acquiesced to the very conventions you challenged for so long?

FH

2.8

Dutch House, OMA

One of the most paradigmatic moments of this house is the moment of entry: you come down the stair and at a mid-point you witness that view, you're not really at the bottom. At the bottom you look down into that pit with the playroom and it's an important moment because it recalls some of the other tropes that we've seen in contemporary and modern architecture—where the ground is not taken for granted, it's an artifice, it's objectified and it reveals an important typological rift in the house but also it establishes a relationship with the landscape—which I believe yours does not. It becomes an incident, it's an episode, it does not reverberate from the inside to the outside and its further exacerbated by the fact that the terrace to which this entire house arguably could have been dedicated is blocked by the layers of infrastructure: staircases and ramps that defer the program that could have engaged the terrace. Why is it that a house, its entire morphology, its entire organization is projected towards this view and that you push everything back? That's not clear.

NT: You recess the programs that could have otherwise enjoyed a more immediate proximity to the outdoors. If it were negligent, that would be one thing, but it seems self-conscious somehow. Why?

I'm coming to the end here. We had, over ten years ago, a discussion at a round-table with various other PA award winners, one of them

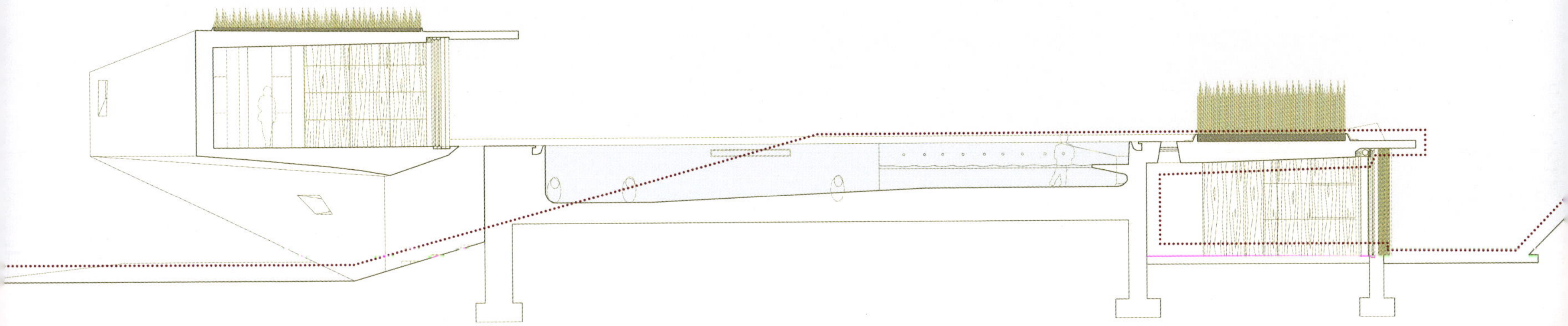

being SHoP Architects. SHoP made a presentation about the Museum of Sex and they made an analogy with a slide of a voluptuous woman with curvaceous forms very abstracted and discussed their façade in relationship to that body and they wanted to make a kind of semantic equation between the two. The next image they showed was the same geometry rationalized through triangulation almost a crystalline form and you went berserk on it. You don't remember this?

PSC: No.

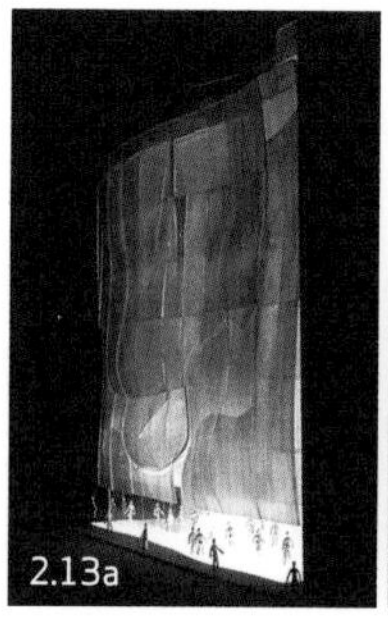

2.13a

2.13b

NT: I believe you were trying to underline the importance of the fidelity of geometric precision in relation to both the semantic aims, as much as the system and rules that guide the project... a frustration with their inability to distinguish the discrete differences between the curved and the faceted, as problems of architecture.

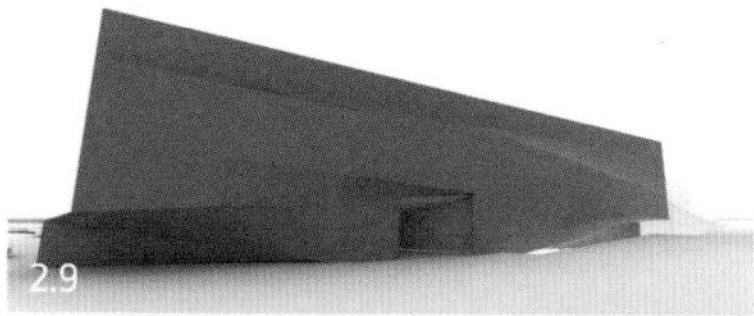

2.9

2.10

2.11

In fact, SHoP's F.I.T. project extends their thinking on MoSEX and eventually rationalizes it with facets. This is something that you also had to undergo in the Tel Aviv Museum; maybe this is how one can describe how you went from the smooth to the discretized, to the fabricated large pixels of the concrete, to the built form. This process of realization, something that you never confess to be interested in within your agency of geometry, has come full circle to deal with problems of aggregation in a more similar fashion to my own biases.

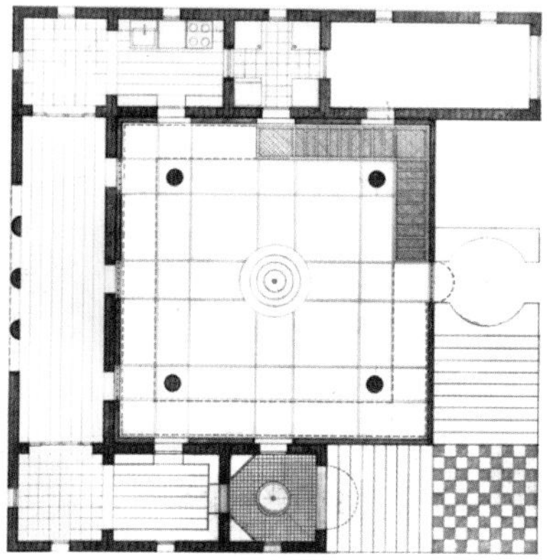

Jorge Silvetti's House in the Island of Djerba, Tunisia (Ground Floor Plan, 1976) and Rodolfo Machado's Country House in Piedmont, Virginia (Piano Nobile, 1977) exemplify a return to typological canons in the 1970s, albeit both with radical transformations to the references from which they emerge.

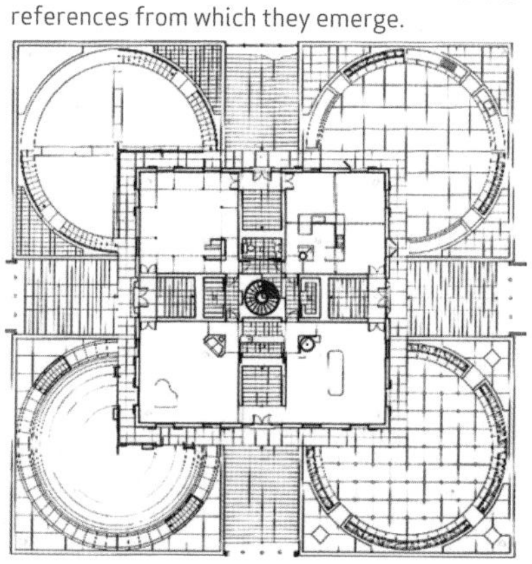

FH

2.12

Finally: How is it that such a deliberate piece of architecture is so casual in its appropriation of an icon? Or the dealing with certain conventions? It's almost banal, almost careless. How is it that a house like this, which is not the result of an existing condition like your Goodman House, built around an old Barn, does not establish a relationship with a new project? And are the windows just operating in a similar fashion, a hap-hazard sprinkling of picturesque openings, or do they amount to something different?

Only one question about this: eyewash or substance? And to end, this is not a question, but merely the insertion of a joker card, in case I get pummeled today. I want one really ugly image to go back to. [laughter]

PSC: ...alright... Nader's house... I think it's a little bit more complex. The site, by the way, is not too dissimilar, but in his case, you enter from the equivalent of the back of mine. If you regard his to be a V-shaped house, he gets in from the concave side. The plaza he created permits us to circle around which is a more beautiful way to enter. The house begins with a kind of originary Rodolfo inspiration, which

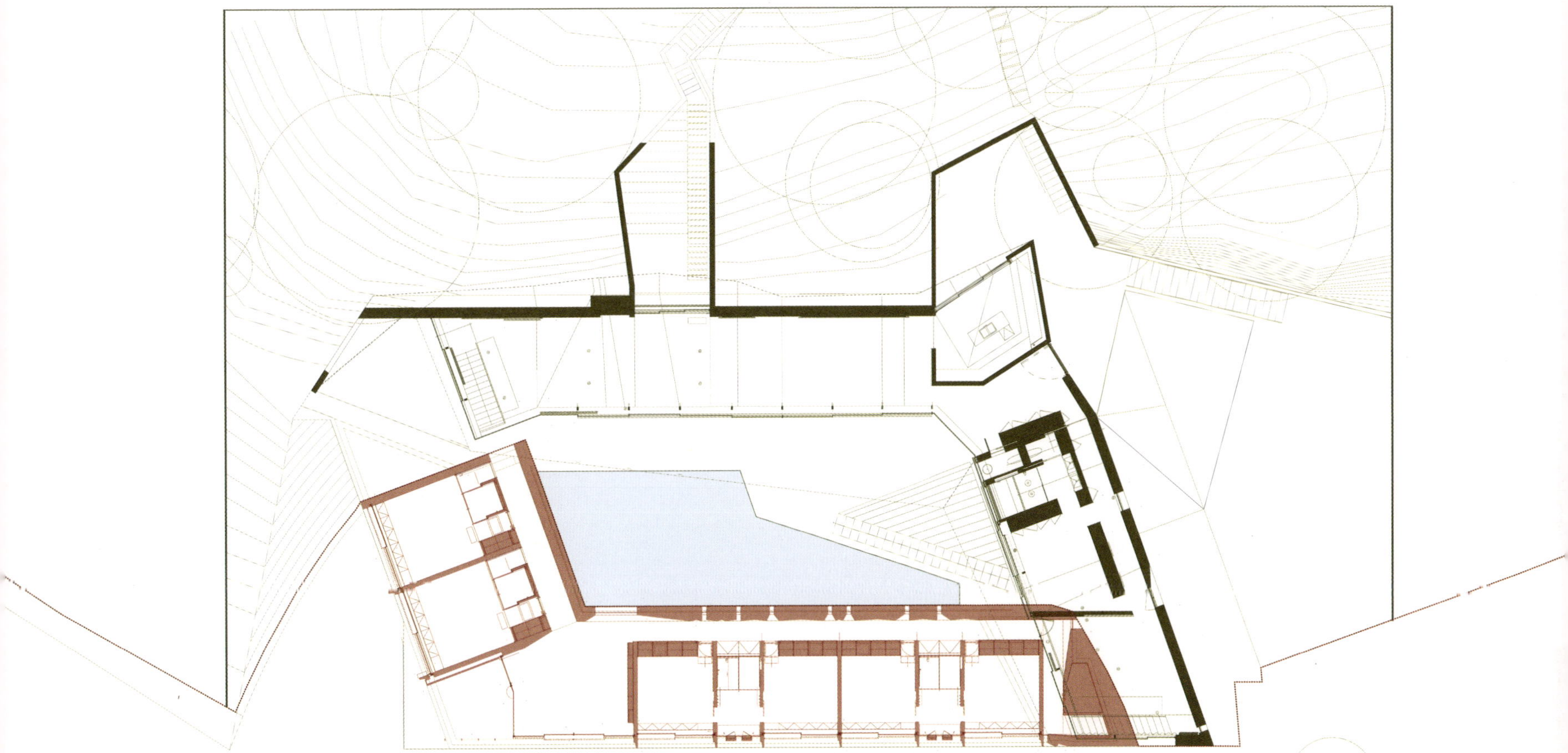

Overlay plan of lower and upper floors of Villa Varoise.

is the sort of linear bar that mine also refers to, but his becomes a courtyard type and the landscape displaces one half of it. He doesn't transform it into a parallelogram by projecting it onto the sloped ground, but he does drop half of the house below the other half. I'm sure some of you have seen how that happens. His distorts it into a parallelogram in plan that will seem directly related to the site. Other things transform it more fictionally—such as where entrances occur and the roof on the other side to let light and views happen in specific ways. And then we see, for the first time here in this animation, something we'll see more of which is an implicit process of change that I believe has some—what should I call them?—physiognomic implications that are also manifest by the animation itself.

The house has two wings. Nader asks that through this very formal wing we will pass to the stair onward to the children's wing. And, on the other side, we may go into a more private stair linking us to the children's wing, as well. I should mention that the children's wing is closer to the parents than the guest part, something that I find so similar to mine where we also have a guest wing set away from the children's room on the lower level.

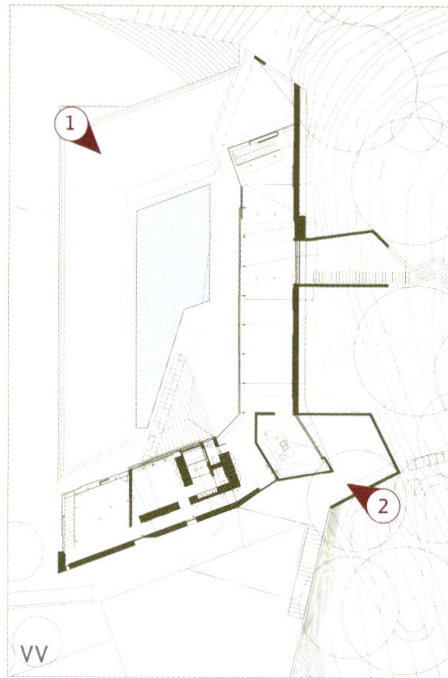

He has a pool in the middle, which is one of the marvels of the scheme because we can actually see the pool in section through windows. I mean, we can actually be below the water itself and view it from the lower spaces. Here's the section of the pool. He doesn't happen to show it here, but there are windows cutting into it. Why didn't you give us a section that cuts right through a window? He complains that I don't have sections, so if I can find anything that he doesn't show in section, it should be considered remarkable, because he's always far more thorough in explaining everything that happens. His representations are always very comprehensive. He rightfully complained to me today that I didn't have what he needed to show and explain my house.

This is the entrance, and you can see the roof overhang, and now we can see the pool.

I want to show you the way his roof moves, which is one of the keys to the project. It isn't part of the originary geometry of the courtyard type, but its operations are meant for opening views to the surroundings. The land itself is traced on the interior. I want to focus on this very interesting scene inside the house. This happened to remind me of another project I'm working on, a museum, where by having one volume rest upon another, there is a similar situation. Incidental-

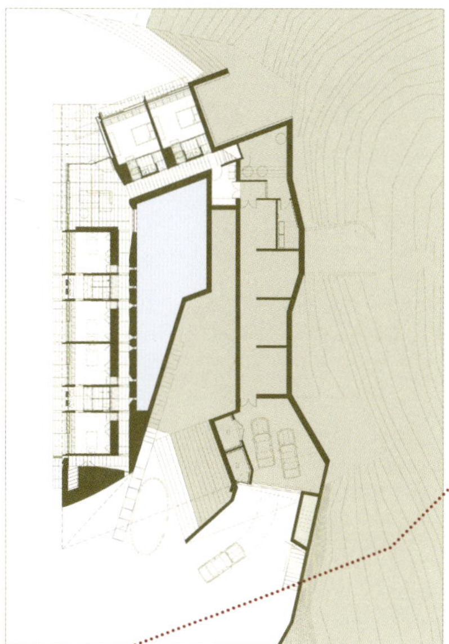

2.14

Taiyuan Museum of Art, Preston Scott Cohen

ly, this museum was designed at the same time as the Fahmy house, so there was something parallel happening between the museum project and that house and I believe Nader's house in particular. We can come back to why and how. Also, I want to point to something he does most effectively which is to allow specific points to connect to the landscape. This is a remarkable development of the interior form which extends into the context.

I wanted to lay on the table something which I think is central to Nader's work that we've been discussing which is that he is very committed to trying to find reasons to invent these remarkable forms that most of his houses possess. I think what he does is to combine representation, what he calls the figure of architecture, with the idea of a certain kind of performance or function. He tries to merge the two and then, in his own way, and I would call it his own style, even, invariably develop the formal result at all scales, not just the general scale of the building.

VV

VV

His work is far more artful, frankly, than mine. It's designed through and through. For example, notice how even the idea of the status of concrete becomes a means to introduce a transformation, in the form of a gradient, from liquid poured into the aggregate of raw material. He wants to show us how he makes his style out of the materials themselves, and out of the circumstances of the site. Certainly, he does not adopt the banal elements that I did in the Fahmy House and leave them as they are. For example, I've complained to him in just the opposite way that he is now complaining about me, about some of his windows, such as the one in the Rural House that results from the rhetoric of cutting black tar paper and those sorts of things. It upsets me to imagine a client being forced to accept having their window blocked in that way. I knew my client never would and that I never would have imagined even asking that they accept something like that.

This raises another issue beyond the artfulness, which is the imposition of art on life. It brings me to the final point in my opening remarks which is that I think we differ on one very fundamental question which takes us back to the debate between Loos and the Secessionists. Strangely enough, that seemed to me the most obvious parallel I could draw from history. Loos did not believe that architectural practice should control all the accoutrements of buildings. Architecture and product design are determined by collective processes that are economically and technically based. The art of the modern architect should be something like the Renaissance idea of "sprezzatura," the art

2.15

of masterful concealment and sublimation of artistic will. In Loos' case, architecture is about the incompatibility of collective values and personal expressions that plays out in the friction between the public façade, a mask that represents anonymity or inconspicuousness, and the private interior, spaces that are richly and individually elaborated. Nader is much more interested in expressing the will of the artist and designing everything, outside and in. I find this most troubling ideologically because I find that the artistic-ness of this kind of totalizing architecture is too solipsistic on the architect's part, particularly with regard to the inhabitants of private houses who Loos thought should choose their own furnishings. And, the architecture of houses differs from that of important public buildings where I believe our obligation is to break from conventions more explicitly, a topic we can follow up on at a later point, perhaps. This is one issue I wanted to put on the table. We can go further as we go back and forth. But I think, first, I'd like you to respond to this point.

NT: First of all, I'm not sure I disagree with your characterization and the problem that you've put on the table. The Rural House contains conventional windows from floor to ceiling—generous by any standards, but with the rubber screen in front of the western elevation, serves as a vertical screen for the afternoon sun. While that is a convenient alibi, the interest in material operations drove the thinking: the formal tropes were the result of material behavior—what rubber membrane can do—and the stubbornness derives from an adherence to this intellectual priority, and it's not typologically driven. But that does not inhibit the performance of the window, not its views, per se. There are ways in which this house can be reduced to a basic barn but in fact it's so specific in its layout and detailing that it's inflexible. In great part and in this house that we're presenting today, not…

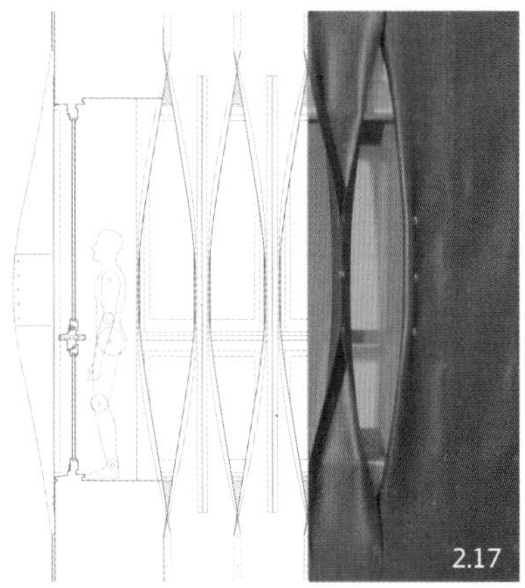
2.17

PSC: This?

NT: No, that's your house.

PSC: Oh, I'm sorry, it's…

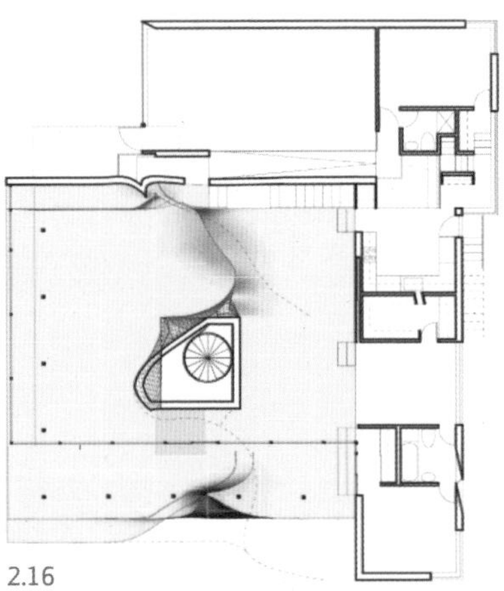
2.16

NT: The house in question [Villa Varoise] is very much a critique of my own prior methodologies, and for me is an extension of those things closer to the Torus House and the Wu House, although I think the Wu House, in part the reason why I see it as an extension of what you have brought to my projects. But this is why I wanted to frame the argument in typological terms and the flexibilities it gives you. If you look at the plan of the Villa Varoise, beyond the parallelogram, it's actually very flexible.

PSC: Let me give a little criticism. You said earlier that, in the Fahmy House, I had not done well enough to exploit everything the sloped ground has to offer. Given this, I believe you probably don't like seeing the ridge cap on this very forward standing seam roof.

NT: Now stay with this landscape, stay with the landscape. Don't go to the ridge roof yet.

PSC: Ok, let's stay with this.

NT: I'm unhappy with it for two reasons. At the practical level you know you have problems with window views being blocked.

PSC: Yes.

NT: Why do you create this huge and great terrace and then only give these two very meager openings that have access to it and the areas that should be more generous to opening to it are blocked and then the main rhetorical landscape move is actually blocking it. It's kind of tackling the house back. At the most "populist" level the way you engage the pleasure of the clients—it's not that great arguably. Hold on. I'm complaining it's not Scott Cohen enough, you should be more extreme. That retaining wall there should not be so banal. It should be a steel blade where the glass floats as a piece of geometry, not as a piece of material. In other words, I'm saying, you're not radical in this way, you're not accommodating in this way, nor are you radical in that way, so what's left over? It's like the middle of the road.

PSC: It's interesting what you're saying about the accessibility of the terrace...

NT: I don't mind the extremity; I mind the middle of the road business.

PSC: Oddly enough, I never considered this to be a building which wouldn't allow people to partake in this space so much as you do, and I now see maybe that what you're saying is true. Given that the whole building is on this topography, it can't let you out easily in any place that we want it to because every time it will do that, the ground has to be leveled, which breaks the bottom of the parallelogram in elevation. So, it's true that I minimized the leveling which makes for having only two narrow doors leading out. But what I liked about this triangular landscaped area is that, unaware, one would discover from one side something that is not understood from the other. It's so inconspicuous as to perhaps go completely unnoticed that this piece of earth, this triangle which appears to be real and merely part of the actual ground, turns out to be part of the house. The whole bent bar is lifted during the concave corner which is the

Fashioned as a case study house plan, the asymmetry of Villa Varoise is the result of the topography. It contains the earth on one side, but the living areas open to the court entirely on the other.

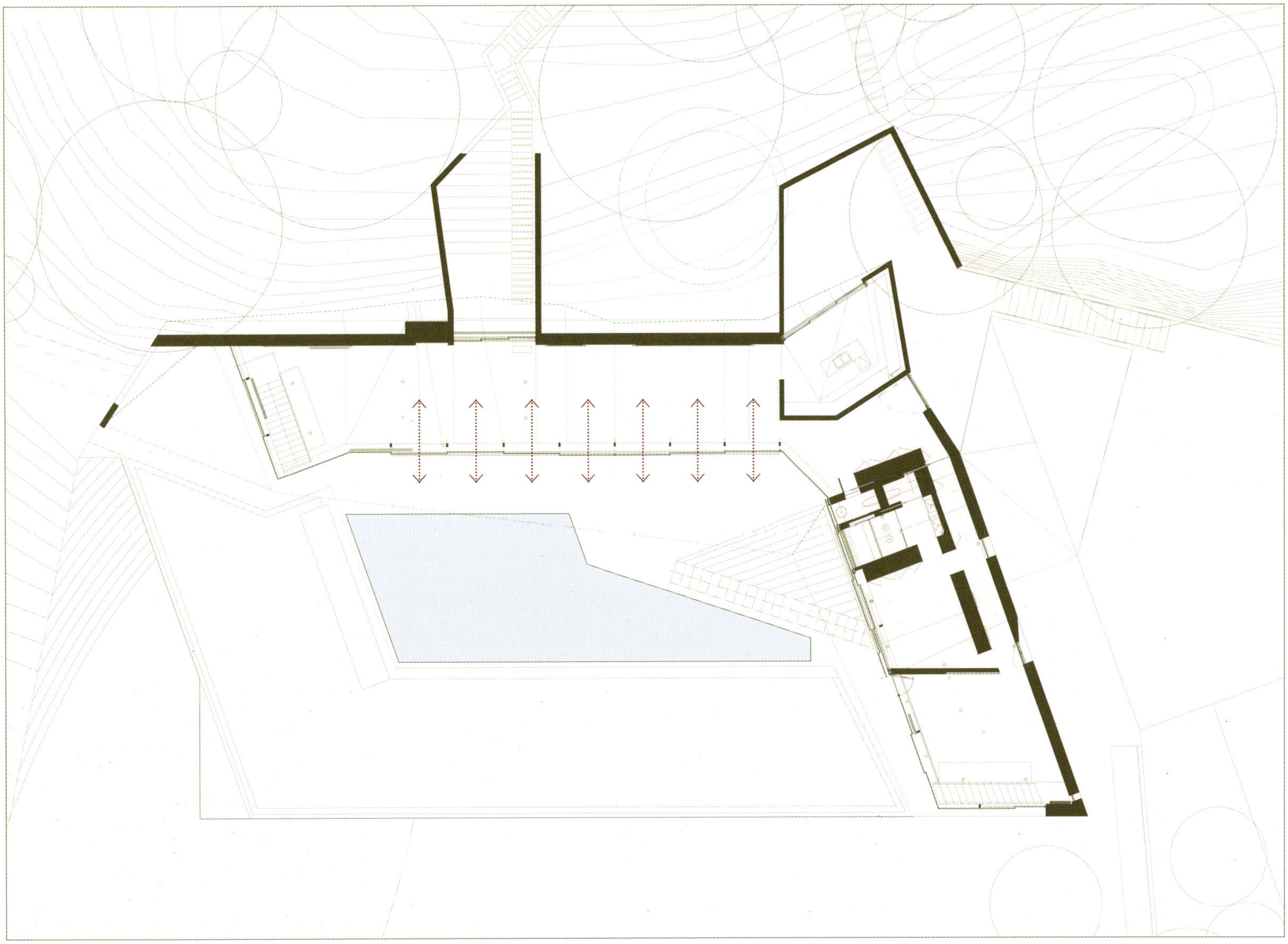

2.18 Villa Snellman by Gunnar Asplund

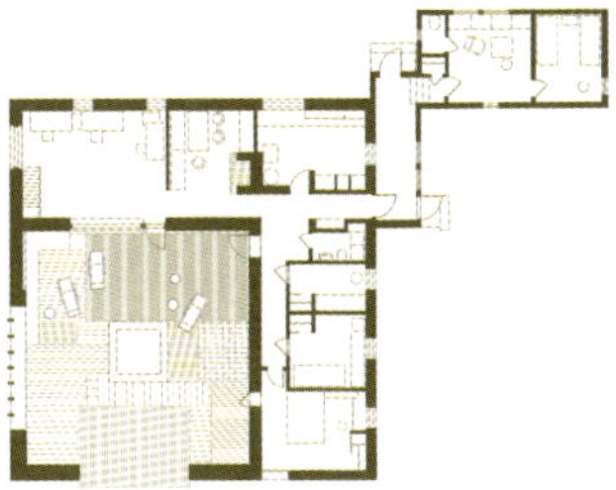

2.19 Muuratsalo House by Alvar Aalto

2.20 Stahl House by Pierre Koenig

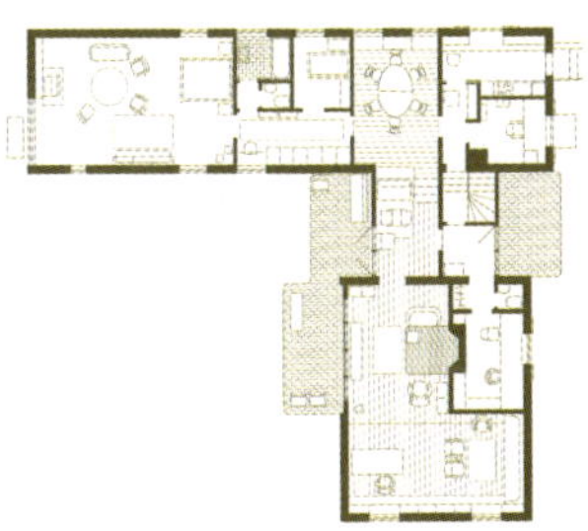

0 5 10m

2.21 Finn Juhl's House

The houses of Asplund, Aalto, Koenig, and Juhl all share the common trait of an "L" configuration that tethers two wings together. If Villa Snellman shows the vulnerability of the corner junction, Muuratsalo instead reveals the power of the displaced courtyard external to the "L". In turn, the Stahl House dematerializes the relationship between interior and exterior to demonstrate the all-important landscape connections between the inside and the out. The Juhl House shows the way in which the entry can be shifted off the corner to allow for visual and circulatory continuities. Villa Varoise draws on all these houses to reveal the tensions at play in the layout of its plan. The two upper wings protect the courtyard from the neighbors' visual gaze, while the entry and kitchen together help to reconcile a complex corner—both *rincon* and *esquina*—to separate the living areas from the master suite.

It is important to note that in the Spanish language there is an a priori distinction made between the inside and outside corner, with the terms *rincon* and *esquina*, allowing them to be infused with not only cultural differences but also theoretical ones that impact architectural thinking.

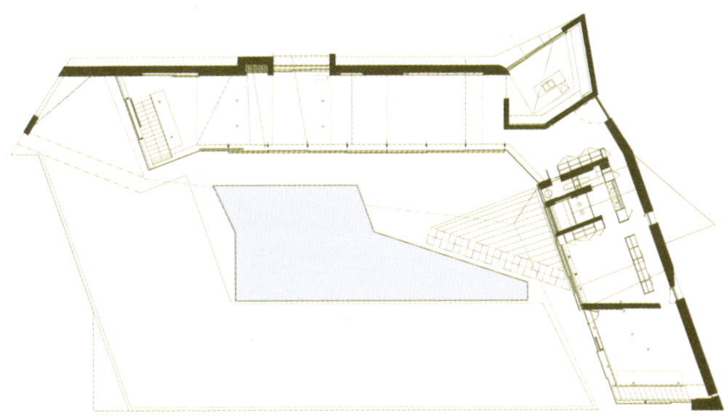

VV

0 5 10m

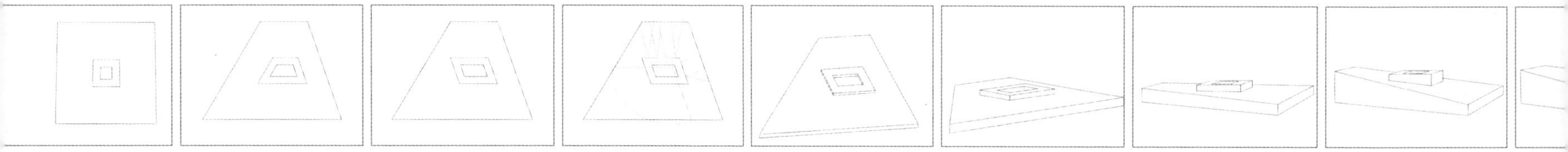

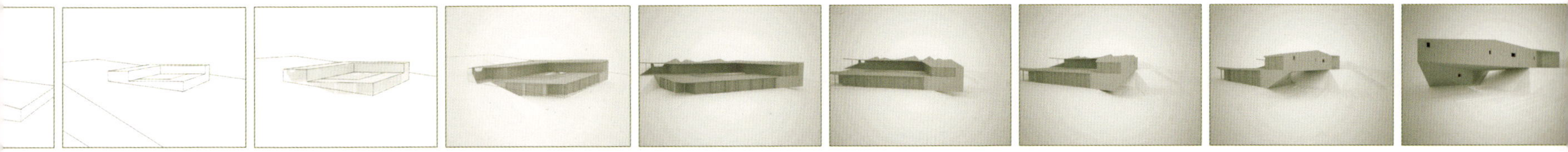

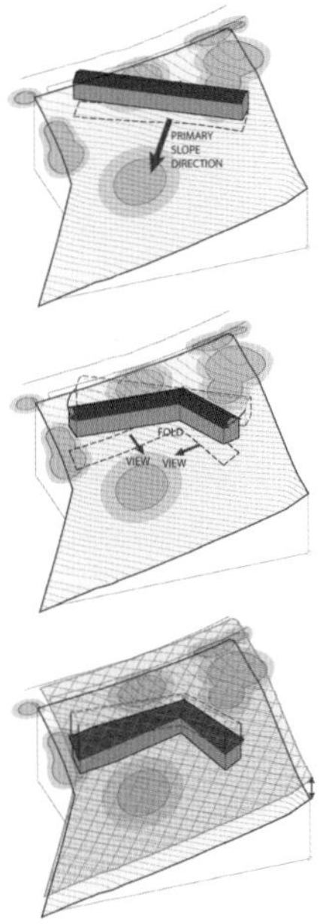

FH

apex of the triangle in question, owing to the force of the bar's integrity. We can see how it lifts, from inside. The bar is not malleable. It is unforgivingly rigid. Therefore, owing to the slope, which pulls its ends down, the folded middle must lift up.

NT: But it's so inconsistent with the kinds of operations that you do that radicalize both geometry, perception, and the way in which architecture engages people. I mean, the retaining wall detail, the way it is drawn, is something you may have seen at the local store in Medford.

PSC: How many houses have you been to where the ground is sloping and forcing the whole house to turn into a parallelogram and in which you discover, inside, that part of the ground is actually part of the inside of the house? In actuality, the interior space is layered obliquely along the hill, with one layer of its interior space below the ground. What interests me about this is both the remarkable behavior of the V-shaped bar that has become a parallelogram in elevation in order to follow the hill, and the fact that you don't recognize what is happening inside and how strange it all actually is. This is what makes it so interesting and architecturally distinguished. Not the style.

NT: It is architecturally distinguished from this point of view. It's just that from the outside…

PSC: You don't know what's happening…

NT: No, you don't, and it's not even that you don't know, it's not even a sleight of hand, it's more like an abdication to convention or to something that the client forced you to do and you said "Ok, fine, I'll just do it."

PSC: Not correct. The client doesn't want this green roof, the expense and problems it may cause. Believe me, this entails a difficult struggle.

NT: It's also such a different track than what you may have done. I'm not necessarily critical of, it's very banal, but you may stake the grounds in them, no? Or may take a—

PSC: What I would like is for the ground around the house to seem so banal, to look so under designed, that it will turn out to be remarkably strange when we discover that it participates in this unusual oblique lamination of interior spaces. In other words, something that appears to be completely innocuous and negligible is actually quite remarkable.

NT: That is an idea that…

PSC: That's what it's about.

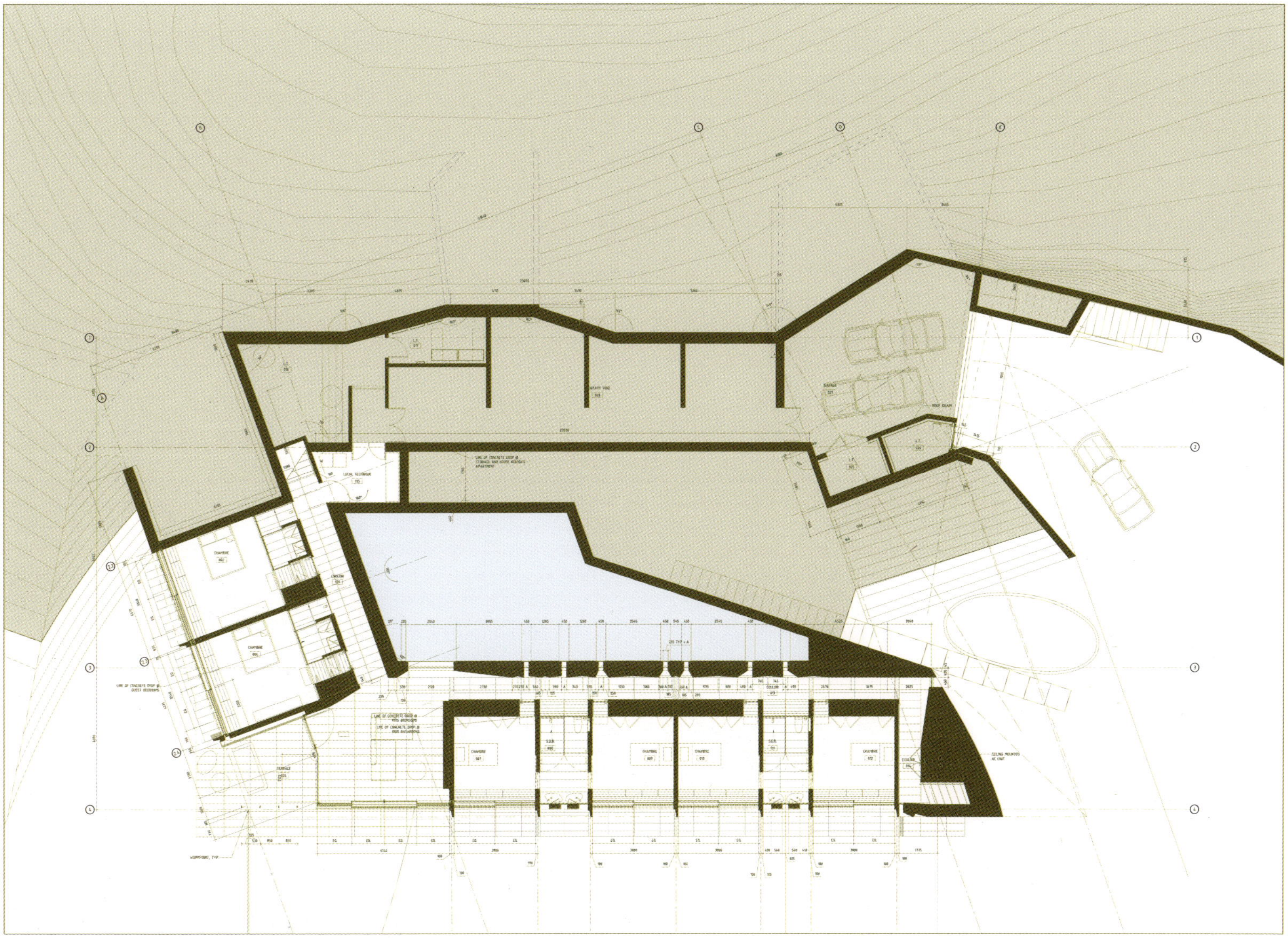

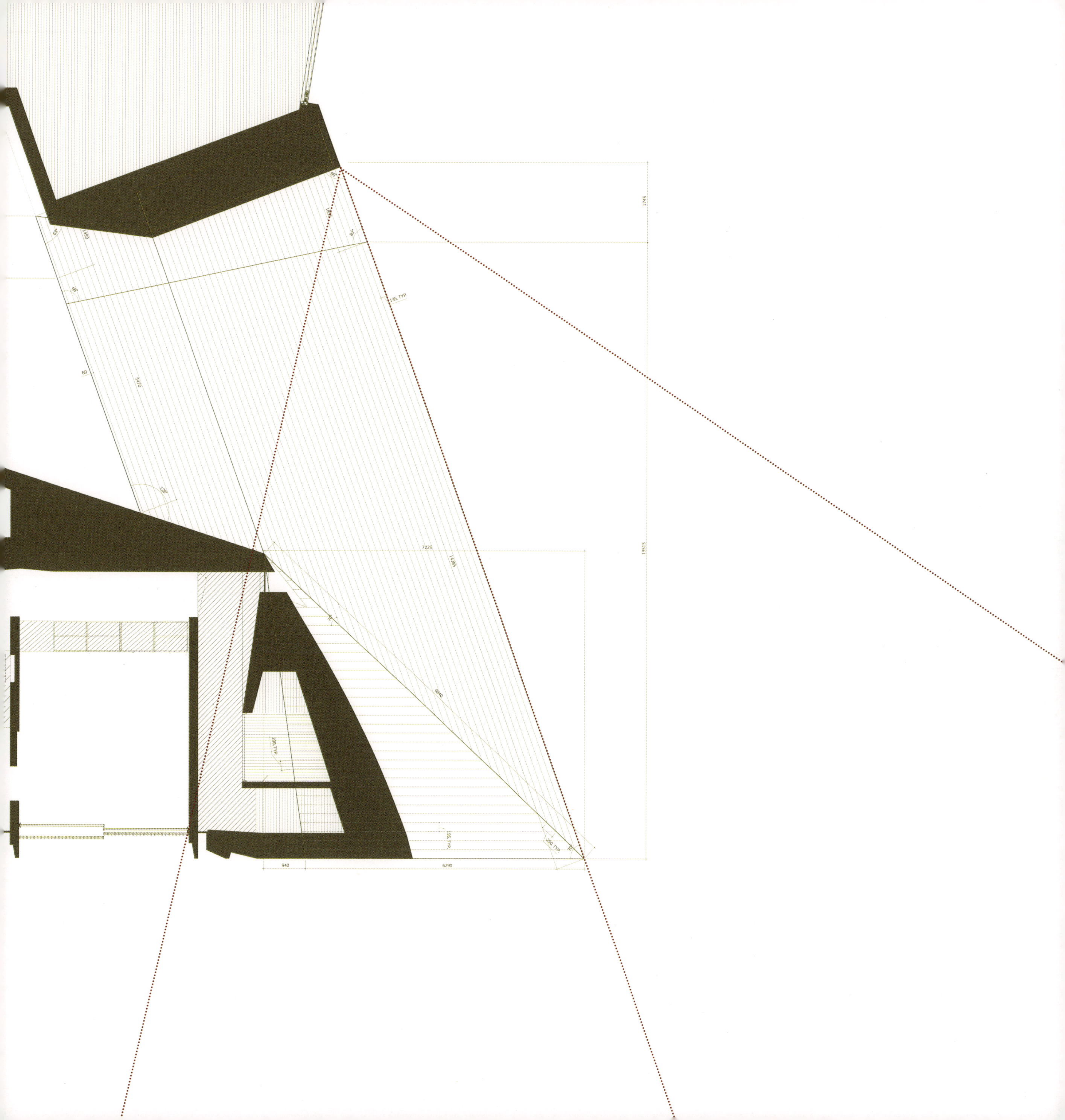

FH

NT: It's also, then you're putting a very strict line between architecture and landscape...because it's also arguable that architecture can leak out into the landscape to the point that it appropriates it in a different way.

PSC: The artifice of that triangle of grass makes it seem utterly indistinguishable from the—

NT: That's right.

PSC: With every way you make things explicit, such as the artifice of your significations, the artful manipulation of your skins, you suggest that you would like everyone to see what you intend and are doing. I would say that you would like people to live with this artfulness, at all times. You're not interested in what I would call, some people are using this word "affect." I'm not going to use it. I'm going to use another word that I like.

NT: I think that some of the people that use that word don't know what they are saying. [laughter]

PSC: I will use two other words: "attention" and "inattention." I'm going to use these terms because I think when you're in the presence of buildings, you're basically in a state in which no one is paying attention, and a situation in which no one is paying attention to what we do. I think architecture, in its basic way of being in the world, requires no attention from anyone. We are to live in it and we are to have our lives predominantly supported by it and I would rather not impose on that. I think that is fine. I think parallel to that, there is another thing going on, an architecture that can be attended to, but this is a project of a very different kind and when the two must come together, I would like to leave the inattentive side of architecture more or less intact. So, despite the fact that the whole house became a parallelogram, the windows are and seem to be merely distributed for the needs of the interior, the particular levels and views. The ground seems to just be the ground as it was found at the beginning. You don't have to bear, at all times, on everyone so heavily with the hand of artistry to make architecture remarkable. I'd rather it be almost unnoticeably remarkable.

2.22

2.23

NT: Fair enough but your entire argument is couched on the difference between a public and a private project here and that's what distinguishes your recent museum in China versus this house. Because the recent museum is—

PSC: That's right, it is different.

NT: The recent museum is so attentive to the entire. Obsessively so.

A

B

C

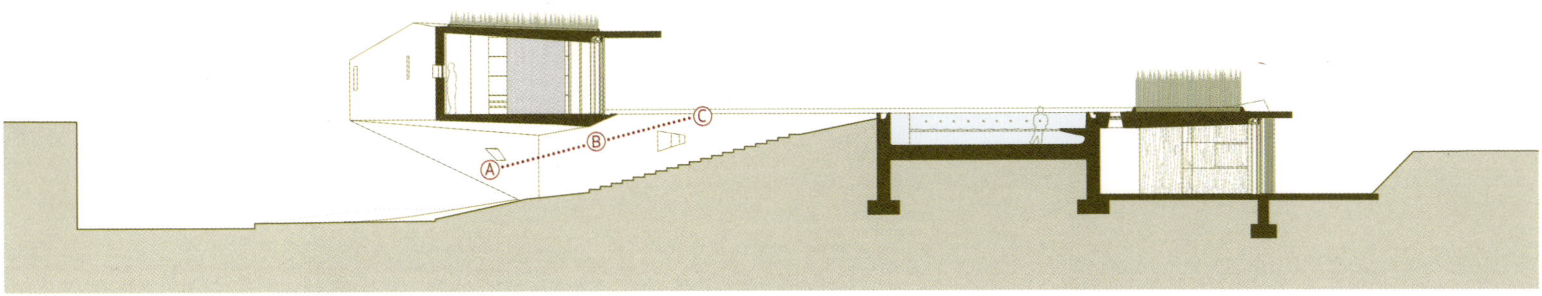

PSC: However, even there, the galleries are left conventional.

NT: Because they took it away from you, Scott. [laughter]

PSC: No, I wanted it. I knew it worked well and I like very much the idea that galleries are able to submit to the curatorial arrangements composed by others.

NT: No, that's different.

PSC: The dialectic between architecture and the normative condition is different in a museum. In a house, the dialectic occurs far more in terms of the question of anonymity vs. the architect's personal or artistic expression.

NT: I was talking more of the exterior of the new museum, where is it? Taiwan?

PSC: Taiyuan.

NT: Taiyuan. And the exterior of the house. Given the opportunity of doing that as a house, in the same way that Rem did the Porto project and the house from which it emerged... Would you bring yourself to the brink of doing a house like that, or not? Would you deny the project? You'd say "no thank you, give it to Nader"? [laughter]

PSC: I don't like it. I don't like to see houses all shapely and artful. And, there are so many of them, by the way.

NT: But would you push it away?

PSC: I would persuade the client not to do that. I've not made a single house where the envelope is an aggressively sculptural project for many years. I take more pleasure in having the envelope be given to me.

NT: So, you're marking a transition from those, but now do you think the Wu house and the Torus House are that kind of self-absorbed, sculptural project, or are they more mediated in their relationship?

PSC: I think Torus House *is blocky and relatively unelaborated as a form on the outside. It has this thing in the interior.*

NT: Do you think the Wu House and the Torus House are as invested in the banality of certain conventions?

PSC: No, they are somewhat more like what you're doing.

NT: They're more like what I'm doing.

PSC: More like your latest house. You, finally, have arrived! [laughter] *But, I think the sculptural forms are a mistake in terms of under-*

2.25

Much like the mule slipper and the mullet haircut, the pickup/coupé is "all business up front, party in the back". Accordingly, the front façade of Villa Varoise displays a civic monumentality while allowing for the informality of the domestic in the back.

2.26

2.24

NT: I should clarify that both the Torus and Wu House have extraordinary qualities that are far more spectacular than Villa Varoise, but they are also derived by certain anomalous projections onto normative typologies. In the Torus House it's the continuous line that emulates the ascent of the spiral stair while remaining completely separate from it, and in the Wu house it has to do with the enfilade of apertures that are the result of the Boolean imposition onto the vaults. These formal tropes do not actually alter the typology of those houses, even if they enhance them. In contrast, for the Villa Varoise, we do not project externalities onto the geometry of the house, but rather distort the house type itself to accommodate the necessary deviations of site and zoning pressures, then resulting in the kind of geometric plays—albeit more subtle ones—that transform the type altogether.

standing domesticity. Now, I prefer seeing the way the stones of the Fahmy House façade are just like any other, but are subjected to this parallelogram formed elevation and thus seem strangely not to be horizontal...

NT: Let me ask you this question.

PSC: Ok.

NT: Do you care, [referring to a misalignment of a soffit line in the Fahmy House] do you care that this line here is not aligned with this? [laughter]

FH

PSC: Yes, I hate that.

NT: And in a public building would that line have just bypassed that?

PSC: It should bypass it here and in a public building.

NT: Really? But you know what kind of structural feats you'd have to do to offset that and what costs and—

PSC: And that's why it didn't happen here.

NT: But you would have done it even in a house? Why?

PSC: I would like to do it in a house.

NT: Why?

PSC: Because I've always wanted to.

NT: It contradicts the very argument you just set up right now. Don't think about what it looks like—think about the decorum of the house and why you would do that.

PSC: Here's the problem with what I'm talking about: I have not said where I would draw the line. Why wouldn't I make the house even more inconspicuous? My own house in Cambridge actually has absolutely no significations of architectural intentionality on the exterior, whatsoever. On the outside, it goes to the absolute end of this spectrum. However, the inside is starting to head into the arena you are asking for. It has several of those exact alignments and tangencies. Clearly, and in that kind of Loosian tradition, the interior of the house is architecture and the outside isn't. Although the way I would program the interior would remain dedicated to the way people would like to live in it and I think you feel that way as well.

2.27

2.28

NT: You know what? The problem is that this is architecture!

PSC: Too much architecture.

NT: I think there's a lot of architecture there.

PSC: Too much.

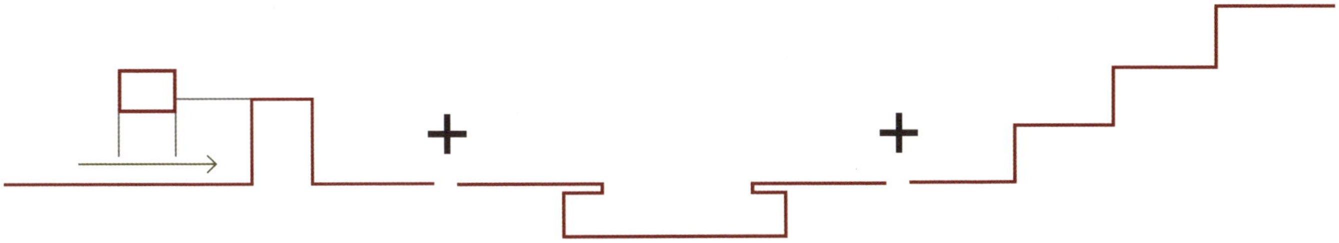

2.29

2.30

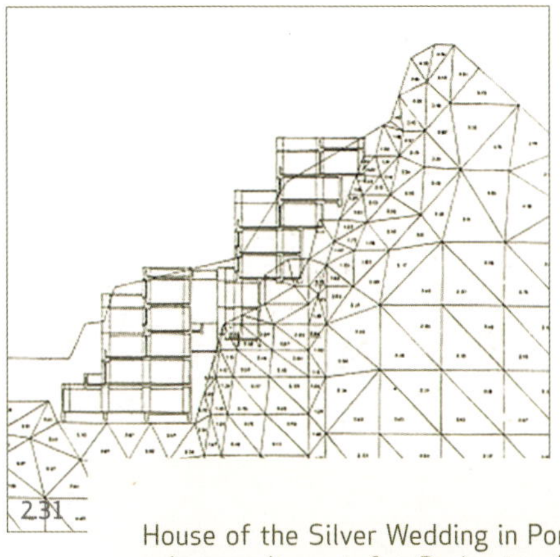

2.31

House of the Silver Wedding in Pompei, Mary Miss's submerged court for Perimeters/Pavilions/Decoys, and Tadao Ando's Rokko Housing project share little in common. However, if taken as separate investments, they conspire to inform something of a different potential when brought together in Villa Varoise. The Rokko Housing displays a technique of how one might build on an inclined plane, stepping each volume up incrementally. Mary Miss reveals the latent ambiguities of the constructed landscape. And the age-old impluvium of the villa in Pompei shows the inner sanctum of a house exposed to the exterior, an inside-out space. Taken together, the Villa Varoise uses the swimming pool as impluvium —drawing in light to the lower floor; its courtyard carving connects it to the main entry to the north; and the stepped profile simply complies with zoning regulations in a strategic manner. Brought together, the three strategies are merged into confluence.

NT: You're guilty of a lot of architecture there. [laughter]

PSC: I'll admit that I can't stop there.

NT: The question is, is it in bad taste? [laughter]

PSC: I want to find out from you, you're the taste-meister.

NT: I'm not.

PSC: I don't really have taste.

NT: No, it's not...

PSC: I don't really care. What I like thinking about is what happened to this house. The fact that it remains, in so many ways, just ordinary, helps me to think about what happened to it, helps us to see that it succumbed to this strange change. For you, everything has to change, or be evidently changed. Why? Why do you need to have everything visibly, perfectly re-designed? Why do you have to design your own doorknobs? Why can't you just buy off the shelf? Why are your windows all custom designed? [laughter]

NT: They're not.

PSC: Yours are.

NT: That's not true.

PSC: Look at this house [Rural House].

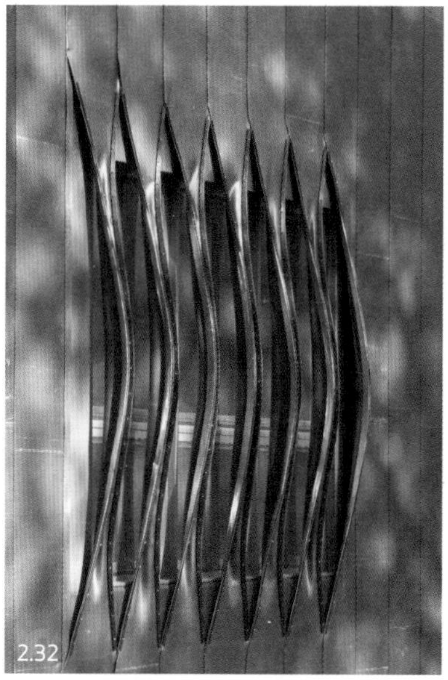

NT: These windows are off the shelf. I work with systems in a very different way.

PSC: But that? Come on!

NT: The windows are conventional.

PSC: But then you hide it.

NT: The sheathing is customized and behind the sheathing is T1-11 which is real, inexpensive stuff.

PSC: But doing that and doing that, perhaps you should only do that on the inside? Why do you need to do it everywhere?

NT: Remember, Scott. I've also evolved in the past years. This is ten years ago.

PSC: Ok

NT: Ok.

PSC: Ok, [laughter] *You showed this the other day. If anyone knows Nader's work, this is his slide, and he was talking about the conceit of hairdos, you know the comb over to the far left on Burt Reynolds and then the actuality of how it's constructed. You are invested in that middle slide.* [laughter] *In other words, I might just do*

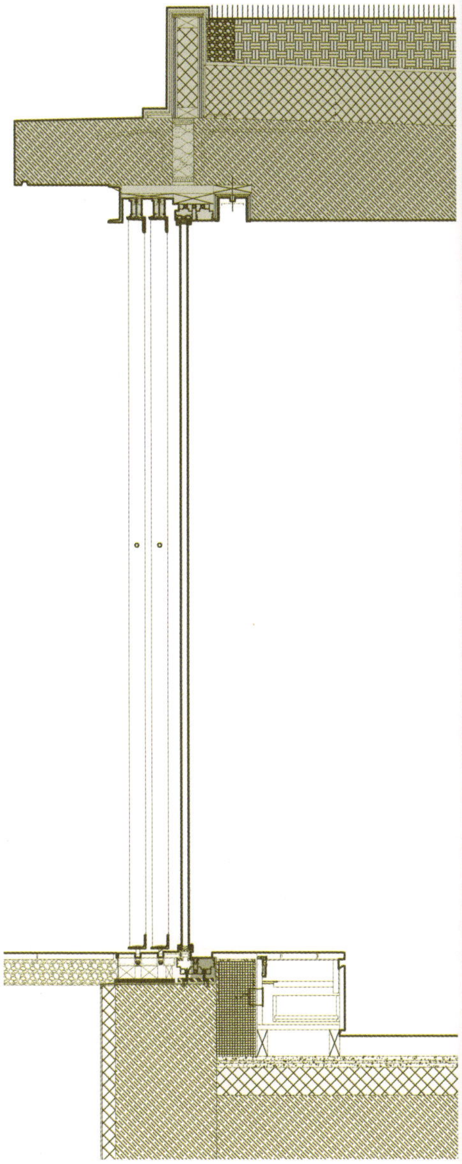

the left side and you would do the middle one. I'm like "ugh, let this house be weird," so that you can kind of tell this is a comb over, but so what? It's the same comb over a lot of people have. Maybe the outside of the house looks a little bit like that, except that it's warped a little too much, and that's what you would call a lot of architecture. Ok? But other than that, it's kind of holding back, it's not going too far. You want to go so much further, to the ontological, internal development of the raw material itself. You want to actually go back to the roots of it and display it, you know, through and through. Why? Why do you need to do that? What's at stake in doing all of this?

NT: Because, first of all, I don't agree that I'm in the middle because the—

PSC: Are you on the right side?

2.33

2.34

2.35

NT: No, not really. They're images that are necessary for the narrative. But on the one hand, it's a kind of critique of denial in the Burt Reynolds slide...effectively the idea that you can't be in denial, you have to somehow deal with it. In the center slide, you get into a point of crisis: the comb-over is so extreme and thin, that it requires structural feats that defy the necessary density of hair coverage itself: pitting performance and symbol against each other. When we get to that point you literally have to glue the hair on with the danger of the wind flapping it to the other side. The third slide is not intended for advocacy, but it shows Justin Bieber's version of the comb-over, long before it is necessary. With a full head of hair, he has internalized an aesthetic, and in turn found a way to support it structurally, such that it stands firm with fidelity. This produces an uncanny condition that I am arguing to be at once self-conscious, anticipatory, and performative at the same time...it produces a new form of knowledge, somehow. That's why these tensions between the image of things versus the actuality of how they perform vary and come into friction. That's where the story is important for me.

2.36
Taliesin West, Frank Lloyd Wright

PSC: Well, I guess in my case, a more modest hope is to have people experience a house in a way they have not quite before, to only subtly push beyond what we know and to have some uncanniness be an end result that may go unnoticed. I want to ask you about what I call physiography here in this picture. I would rather the building look like a normal building as much as it possibly can and yet still be interesting, to make it as interesting as possible for architecture itself but maintain its normality to the extent that I can. In contrast, you would like to change the image of architecture, move it to-

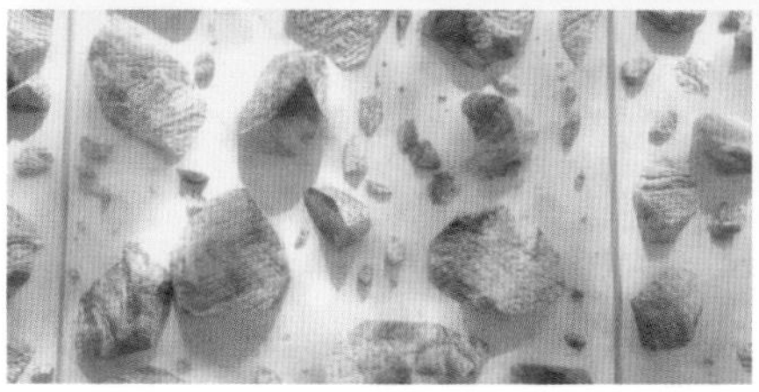

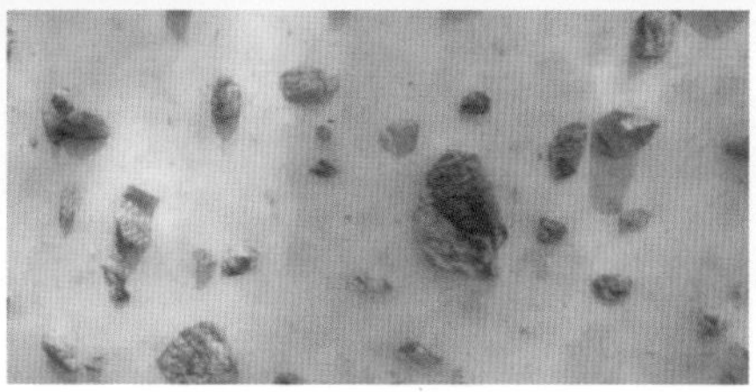

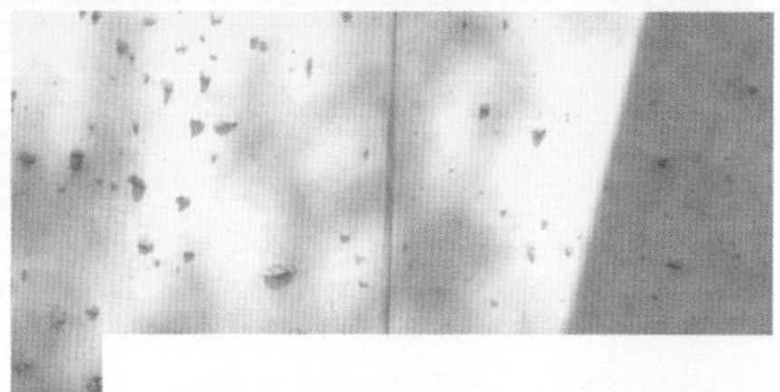

Concrete construction relies on a poured composite system of construction, defying the traditional aggregation of elements as is customary of masonry walls, timber frame, or steel stick construction. Still, it is the aggregate within concrete construction that gives it variability, body, and intelligence. It can contain fine or coarse aggregates in combination with Portland cement; however, with admixtures, polymers, or lime-based binders it can add differences in strength, curing and behavior. Of these variables, if the aggregate base is seen as a critical protagonist, then it displays the ability to develop a series of poured panels whose aggregate size might vary from the minute to the colossal, allowing for the transition of a smooth concrete wall in the interior to a rustic stone wall in the landscape. Frank Lloyd Wright's Taliesin West, and Rafael Moneo's Kursaal project both deploy the large aggregate strategy with effect, but both tend to naturalize it as a stable construction convention. For the Villa Varoise, we had wanted to challenge the perception of this medium through its variability.

2.37

2.38

2.39

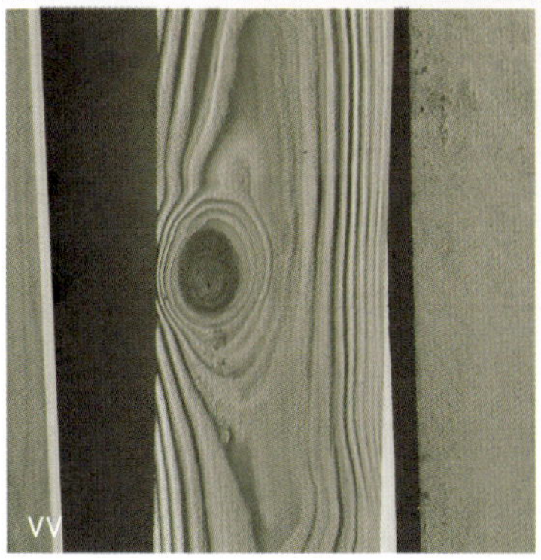
VV

VV

VV

As a liquid-based medium, concrete construction most often relies on its formwork as the basis for its expression. The vessel that contains it is what ultimately telegraphs its surface onto the concrete, giving it the smoothness, depth, or texture it acquires. Bush-hammering is also a well-known technique that is undertaken post-pour, giving a more rusticated finish. In working with the local earth of the region, we found the aggregate to be naturally very warm, giving the surface of the concrete yellow-amber hues. To reinforce this, we developed mock-ups to enhance the latent ambiguity between concrete and wood, by developing a sand-blasted board-form framing, allowing the depth of the wood grain to mirror itself onto the concrete—effectively bringing them into semantic alignment.

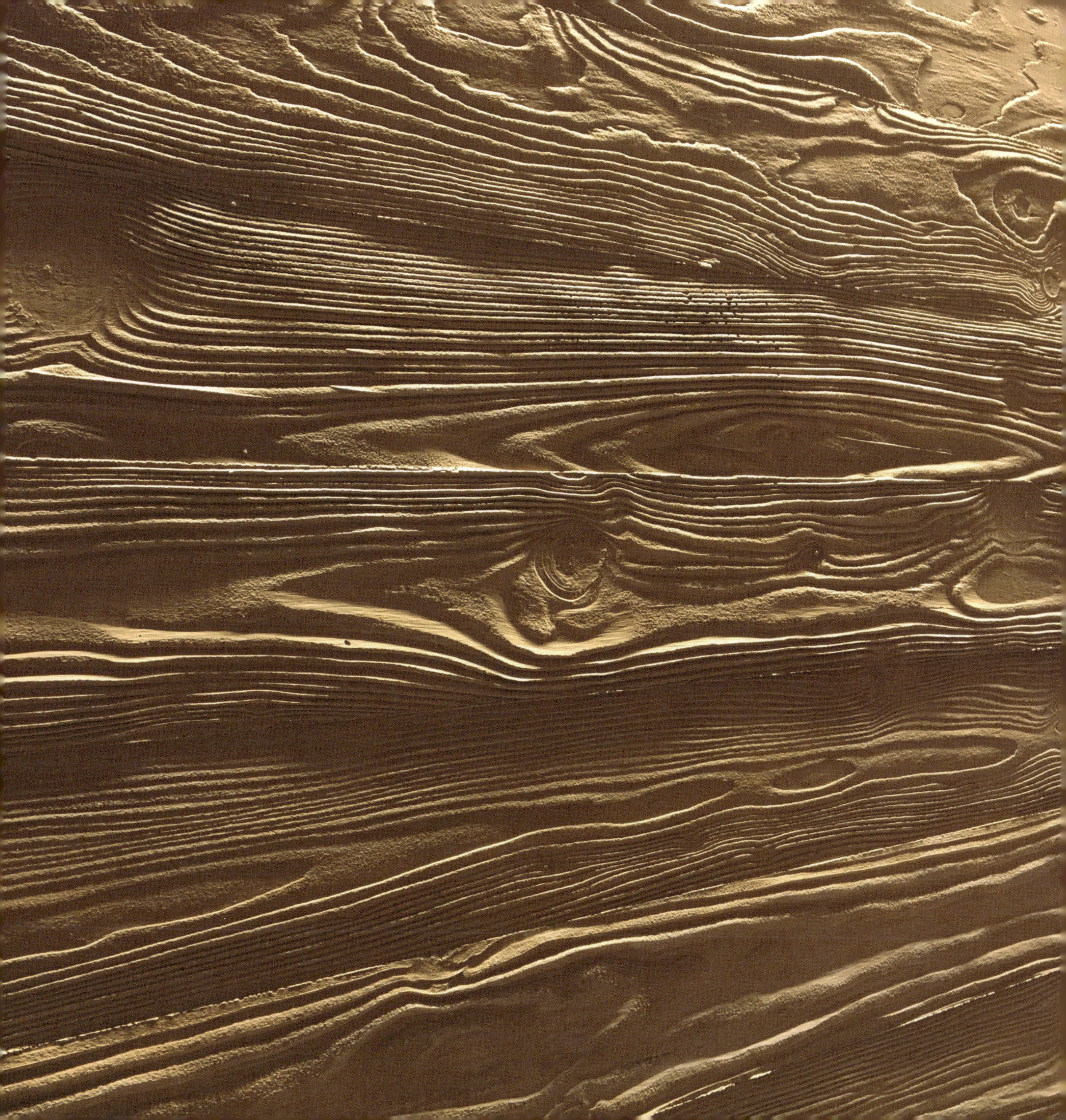

ward a kind of physiography.

NT: I'm not, I'm not exactly sure.

PSC: You're more physiognomic, yes.

NT: To the extent that physiographic and physiognomic strategies are fundamentally different, I think it important to clarify them here in the architectural context. In part, it reminds me of FOA's argument of the 1990s where they attempted to escape the figural connection between their Yokohama Terminal building and its wave-like appearance, making reference only to the metric variations in section as "objective" circulation data, as if the project was an embodiment of a geographic pattern, rather than a figural desire of authorship. We know how that ended, and their own text on The Hokusai Wave is an acknowledgement of their own denial. In contrast, my claim is that the physiographic and physiognomic are deviously linked together in my work, because of the way I work deductively and inductively: I anticipate figures that are the result of patterns, while also searching for inventive modes of organization that have the ability to produce unanticipated forms.

NT: So, as we are getting to that point, why is it that you're putting so much attention to the lintel that gets you across when you know that the lintel is not necessary to build this because it will be built with a kind of—

PSC: Because it's a conventional style, it's straightforward.

NT: Well it could have been all stone. Use the stone, the same way you photoshop the stone, you could just photoshop it all the way across. [laughter]

PSC: But the more conventional treatment makes it go away more than total abstraction does.

NT: No, it doesn't, it puts an eyebrow on everything. It says look at me I'm architecture: I'm spanning, look at me spanning.

PSC: Yes, I'm architecture. Yes, in a very conventional way, this is the way we make a window.

NT: Can you tell me what the wall section of that looks like, i.e. How does it actually span?

PSC: Well it's thermal—

NT: No, it's not thermal per se. It is a structural question. It's different when you have a concrete beam as lintel versus a steel angle, and this could be a steel angle that holds the stone on top of it without expressing its structural function. So, it does make a difference.

FH

PSC: It does. The only question that I have—

NT: Don't you agree?

PSC: Whether the stone and windows should slope?

NT: The stone should slope? Which stone should slope?

PSC: It could have sloped with the parallelogramic form of the whole elevation—

NT: Oh, but that's like me, that's architecture again, you're slipping into my paradigm.

PSC: And it did that, at one point, and I stopped it. [laughter...] *This is what I like about it. The geometry of these wings is holding rigidly and will never allow this middle area to bend. The parallelogram in elevation is so rigid that it forces the inside to adapt. You can see the middle lift, because it can't let go and fall. From the inside, the exterior façade acts like a given. Imagine*

2.40

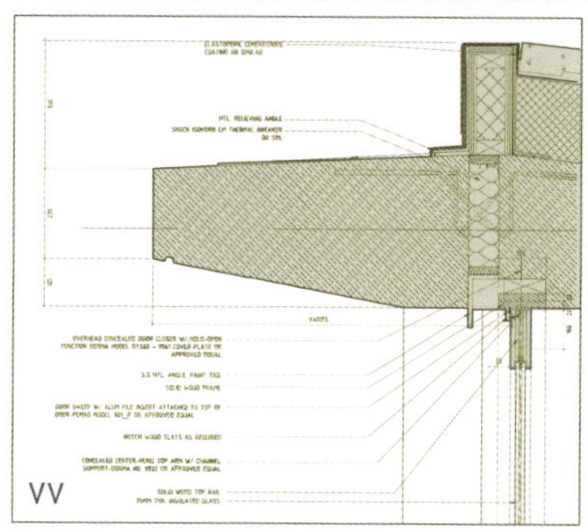

VV

the givenness of a pre-existing building and then an interior that is developed for it...It's as if some of these relationships occurred involuntarily owing to the rigidity and integrity of the exterior form. I like this type of problem and imagine you do too.

NT: Ok, let me show you in an instant. Why is it that you force your cornice line to be absolutely straight from beginning to end when in fact it could have been a conventional building? It goes there and it goes down and it goes like that, it could have been messy. Look at this house.

PSC: Yours is much messier.

NT: It's messy. You know why it's messy? Because I took the type all the way across and then the zoning pushed it down and went "khehtt."

PSC: Ok, because if you don't go "khehtt." If you hold on to the shape, you don't have to do anything else. It's so remarkable that it does what it does, even if you leave the stone banal, leave the windows banal, leave the rooms banal. They all do something unusual because of the conflict.

NT: When your client wants more real estate, you have to leverage every little bit of space and extend it out and it goes "khehtt," that's why. If you wanted to maximize the FAR and get the maximum height at certain areas it would not have necessarily produced a straight line. What I'm challenging is whether that line actually does need to be straight or if that's an architectural conceit.

NT: The roof topography is dictated, in part, by the slope of the land. Houses as viewed from historic landscapes across the valley must blend visually with the surrounding landscape and vernacular architecture. The project's zoning restrictions included a maximum gross area of 500 meters-squared, maximum height of six meters between the lowest eave on the upper roof and the finished floor of the lower level, and a maximum height of six meters between the top of the roof and the existing natural landscape grades.

PSC: The unforgiving straightness is an architectural conceit, absolutely. That's my conceit. I reduce the architectural conceit to this one thing so that everything else can be normal while you continuously produce conceits and differences, newness and artfulness everywhere, all the way down to the handle in the room. That's the difference between us.

NT: There is a difference between us. This house is pretty restrained in the context of...

PSC : It is.

NT: I spent twenty years building up an argument and now I'm editing it.

PSC: Ok, now I need to get editing and stop doing this in public buildings, too. Alright, let's hear from people with questions. Carl?

Audience [Carl Dworkin]: What I heard you say about the fact that you can't access the terrace in a normal way makes me wonder if this is the point, actually. The fact that there is this infrastructural buildup of ramps and stairs and that

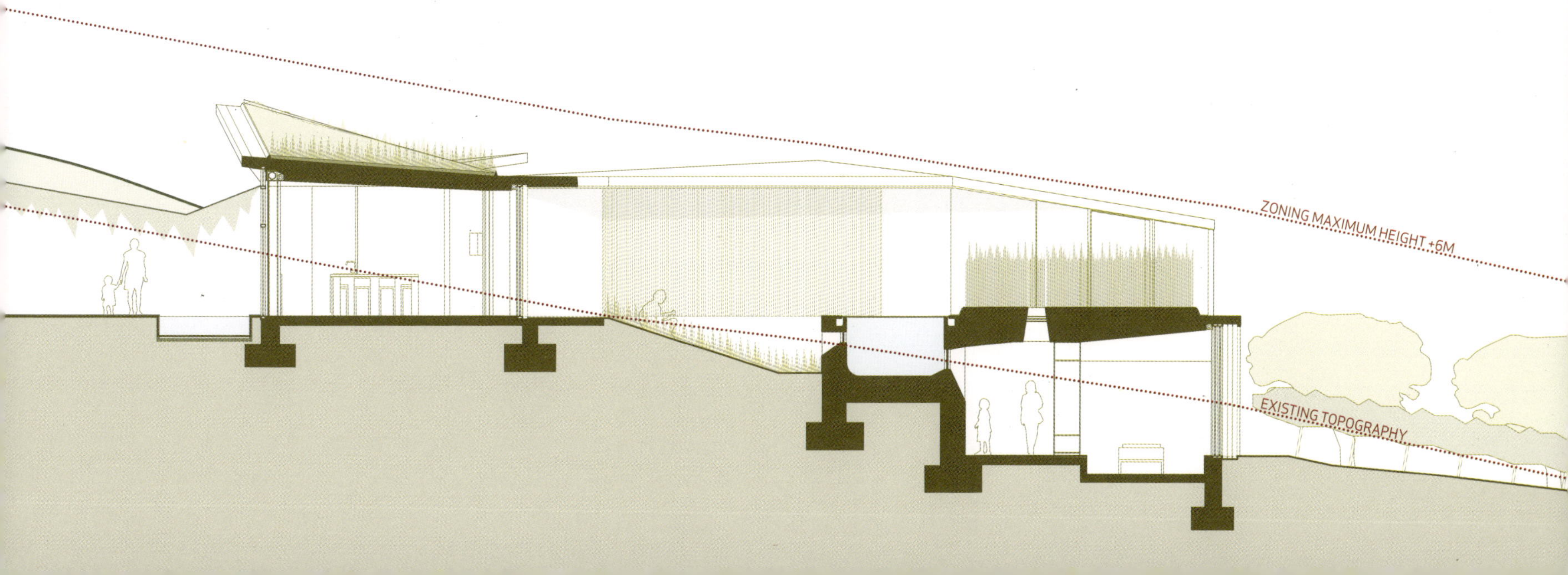
ZONING MAXIMUM HEIGHT +6M
EXISTING TOPOGRAPHY

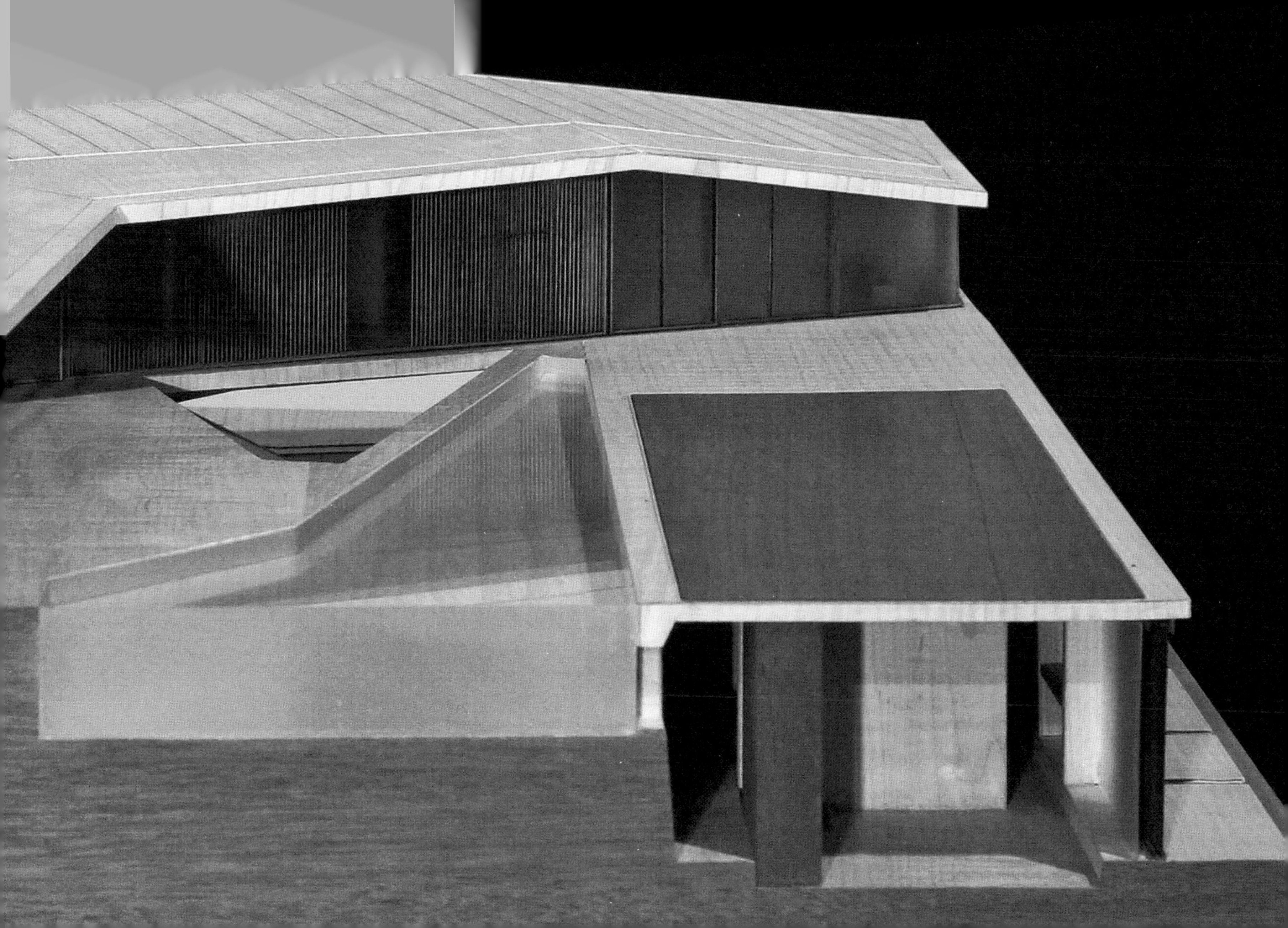

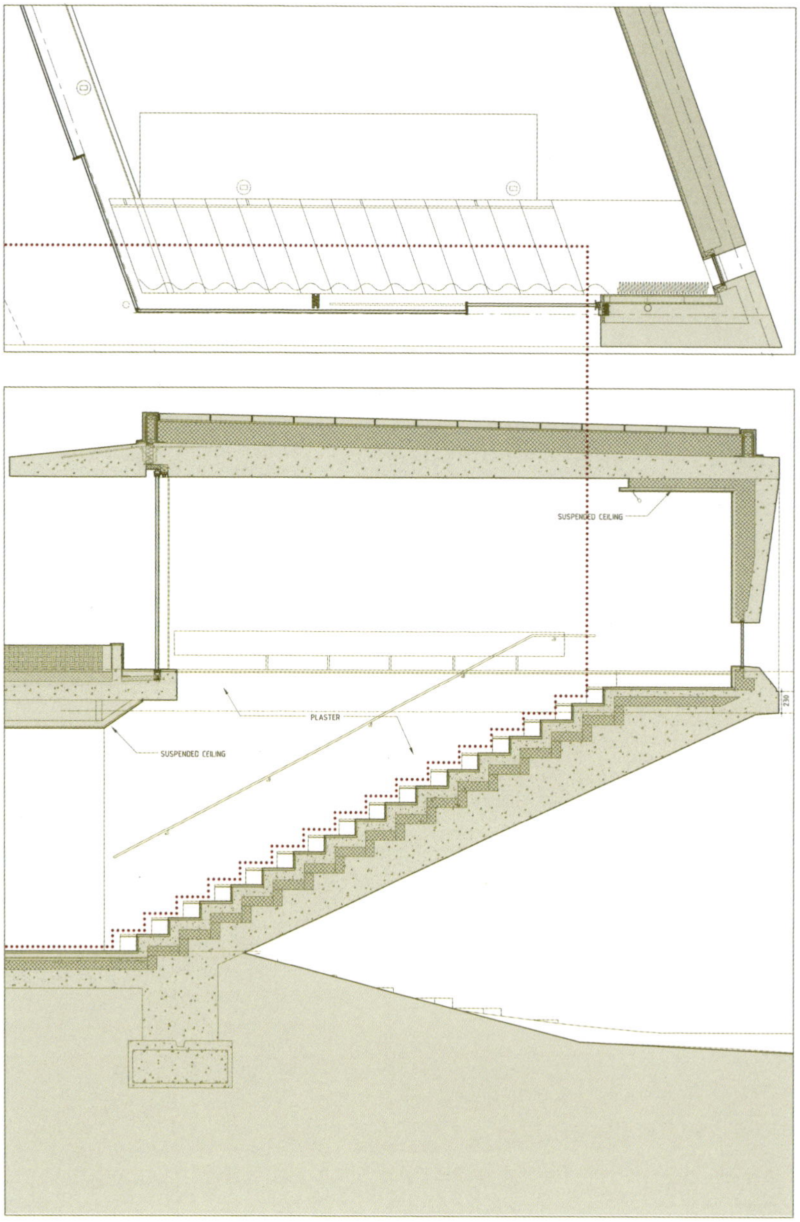
SUSPENDED CEILING
230
PLASTER
SUSPENDED CEILING

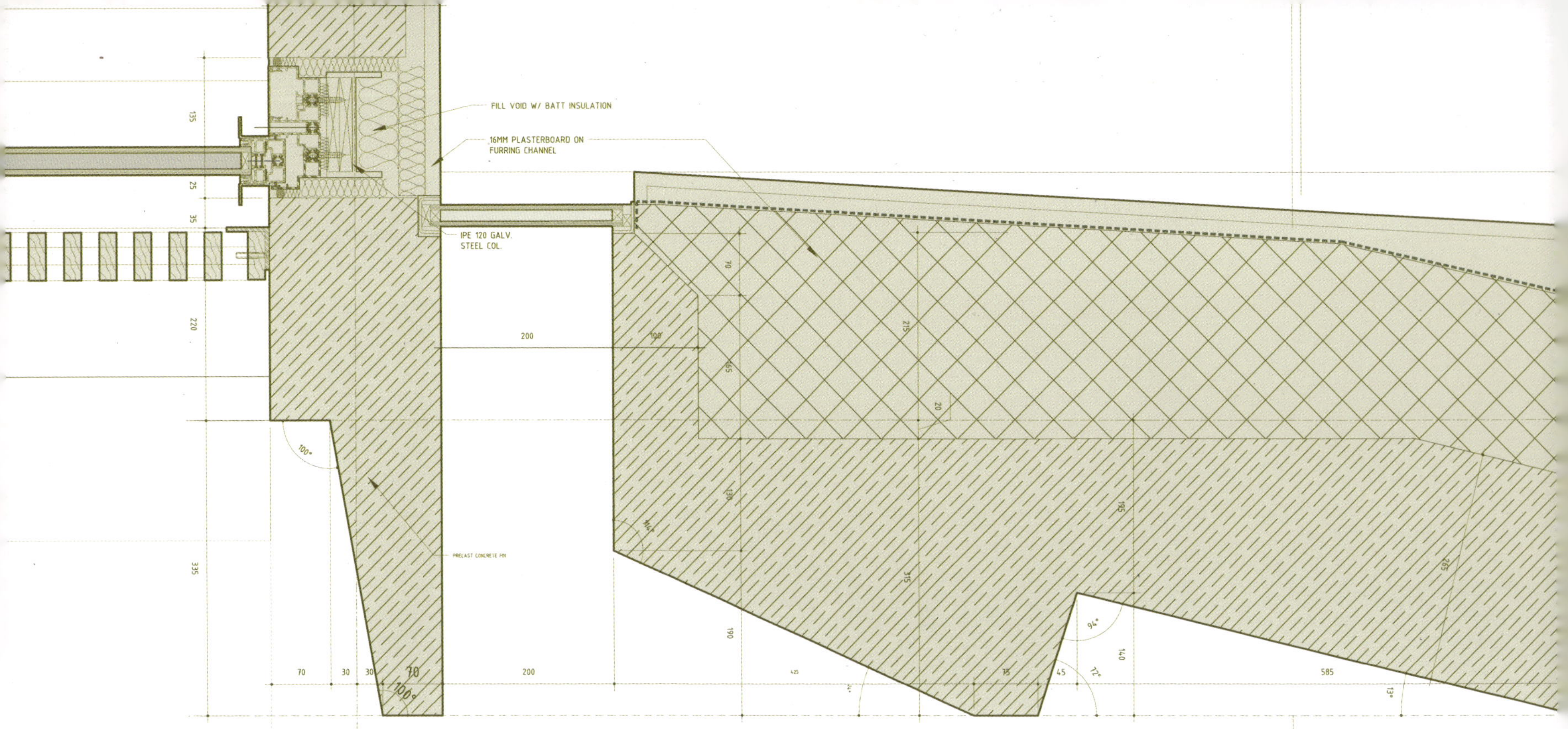
FILL VOID W/ BATT INSULATION
16MM PLASTERBOARD ON
FURRING CHANNEL
IPE 120 GALV.
STEEL COL.
PRECAST CONCRETE FIN

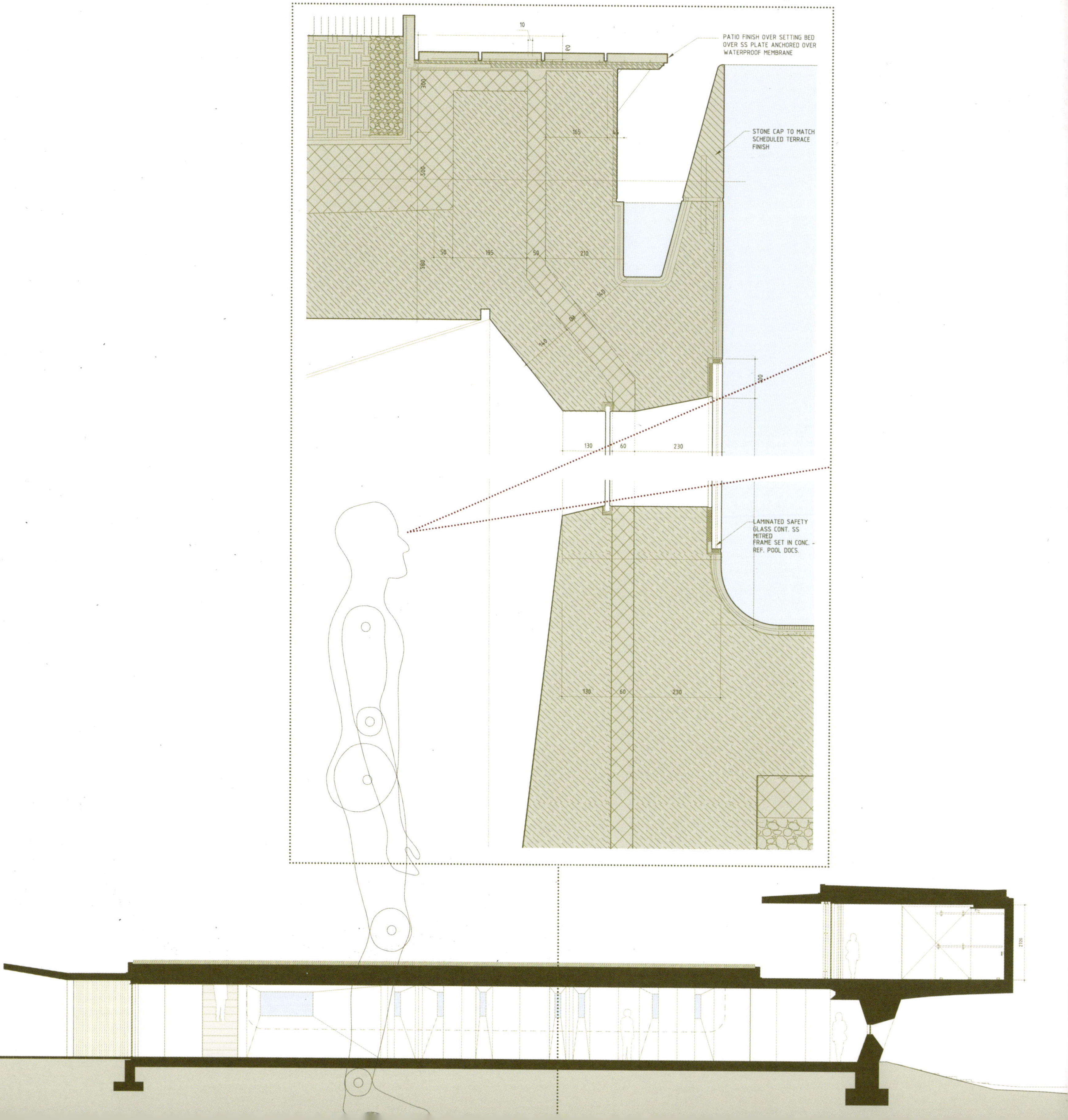
PATIO FINISH OVER SETTING BED OVER SS PLATE ANCHORED OVER WATERPROOF MEMBRANE
STONE CAP TO MATCH SCHEDULED TERRACE FINISH
LAMINATED SAFETY GLASS CONT. SS MITRED FRAME SET IN CONC. - REF. POOL DOCS.

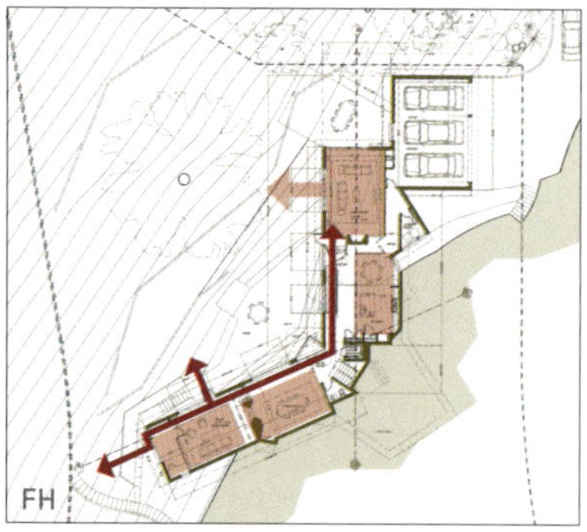

there's only the single doors onto the terrace, rather than a whole bunch of doors, suggests that the house is in the process of losing its house-ness. It's becoming like a larger scale building, in a way, because the skin is independent and we have only these single points of entry and there's infrastructure in the building which doesn't belong to any one of the rooms of the house. So, in a way, the house, while it looks like a house, is beginning to behave like an institutional building.

PSC: That is extremely interesting. The problem is different when you're working with something like an 18th-century Dutch Barn or a 19th-century worker's house in Cambridge. When you try to create this quality of typological givenness in a new form, in our time, it is always arbitrary and abstract. There's no such thing as a house that everyone agrees looks like a house except for the most cartoonish and reductive gable form. As soon as it becomes abstracted, it moves toward what you're describing, something not domestic. It happens that the adaptations to it on the inside, such as the ramps which are needed to navigate the parallelogram formed volume, clearly are not what you would normally have in a house. It's true that these elements do not participate entirely in the conventional language of houses. That's the irony of it, you see. It's pushing and pulling toward and away from the conventional. It's conventional and nonconventional. It's about conflicts between aesthetic and practical codes. I'm interested in conflicts between codes. I think Nader's is more synthetic. There are conflicts between codes in his too, but they're much more synthetically resolved. The house is more integrated and more resolved, as I've already said, through and through, from its form to its details. Mine is more unresolved and rough-edged, which maintains the tension. Yes, Inge?

Audience [Ingeborg Rocker]: I have a question. How happy are you with the eyelashes, not the eyebrows, but the eyelashes in your building?

PSC: What eyelashes? You mean the dormers?

IR: Yes. I think they are ultimately a stylization of the conventional. This is a problem because that's where the normality couldn't be executed. This treatment resolves the tension between the normal windows and the odd geometry of the other normal, the façade which is distorted. That resolution had to take place here again in a vernacular which I think is rather clunky.

PSC: So, you're saying that my efforts to make it look vernacular have gone too far? Astray?

IR: Astray.

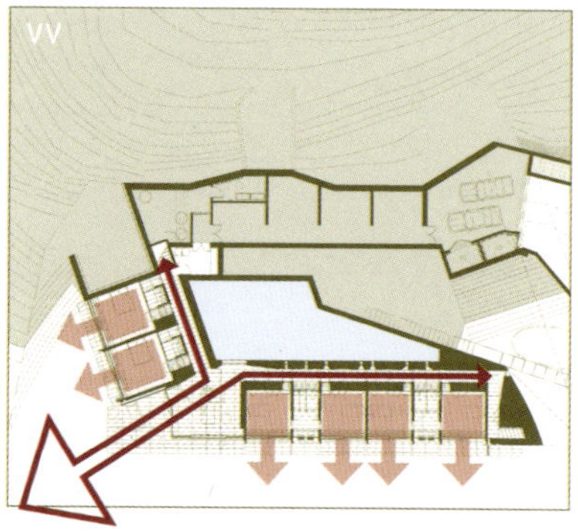

The lower level of Villa Varoise contains a second living room on the southeast corner of the house, offering it a prime view of the Mediterranean beyond. As is emblematic of the bedrooms also, this space is designed to establish a meaningful relationship between the inside and outside. The stone floor of the room extends outside seamlessly, registering the geometry of the eastern wing from which it acquires its tectonic grain. A sliding glass door slides back entirely; its tracks embedded in the floor, the continuity of the landscape is given priority. A slatted board-and-batten teak wall on the west extends the materiality of the interior into the porch. Much of the daily life in the Mediterranean is done outside, and thus, these spaces offer a level of flexibility to allow for ample shade with natural ventilation being drawn into the interiors.

PSC: It should be more abstract or even more ordinary? What do you want?

IR: Well I think that, it's a funny thing, because I'm not conflicted with the landscape. I think that it's doing the intellectual twist you are interested in. What Nader feels, I think, is that it needs to remain a straight line in order to have the normality that he wanted in order for it to be architecturalized. See, for me, these dormers break it and are that odd in-between where it is architecturalized and yet evoking a vernacular.

PSC: Oddly, my answer to you would be—and you're not going to like this—that I don't really care about it much. Let me tell you what interests me more.

IR: Oh, you cared a lot about this.

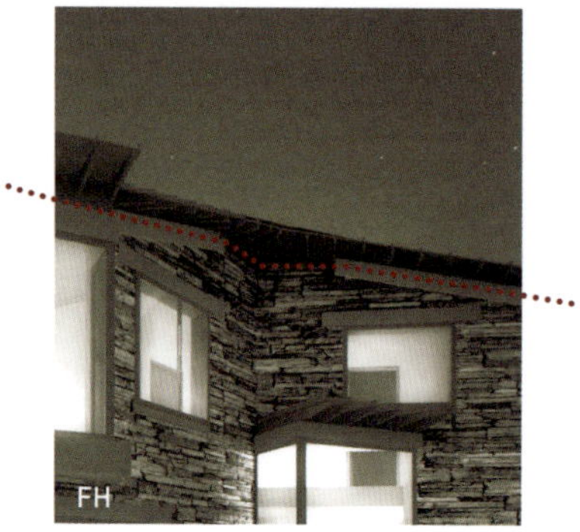

PSC: Let me explain something. The roof comes to a perfect apex right here and because the walls are set back from the apex, this wall must bend down—this is the one time there's a violation of the parallelogram, because if you pull it out flush, you'd have no overhang. In order to have both the apex of the roof be at that point and have these parallelograms remain pure, an overhang forces a betrayal of this parallelogram and in betraying it, forces this whole wing to be a giant lintel that stops just prior to that violation. The violation makes something remarkable happen. It doesn't matter if you like or dislike it, or if you have a taste for more abstract or less abstract stone. I don't care whether its ugly vernacular or more refined and tasteful abstractness. It's what happens when whatever it is in crisis that interests me.

IR: Yes, but this is not a crisis. This piece is not a crisis. This is what I call the eyelash, and I would say this one is not really in crisis.

Audience [CAMERON WU]: Why do those windows need to be popped out proud?

NT: They're on the other geometry, they're on the orthogonal geometry that's perpendicular to the topography.

PSC: There are two ideas about these push outs. It's true that this is just willfulness. I will concede that they are an attempt to flatten the house. They are a holdover from an earlier obsession with projection. If you look at the rear elevation, they are frontal despite the insistence on the v-shaped plan that all the other windows reinforce. These four windows are absolutely frontal, the ones with the eyelashes, as Inge calls them. It's almost an anamorphic phenomenon. On the interior, they do something rightful in the plan. They orient you, such as where you come down the stairs and one of

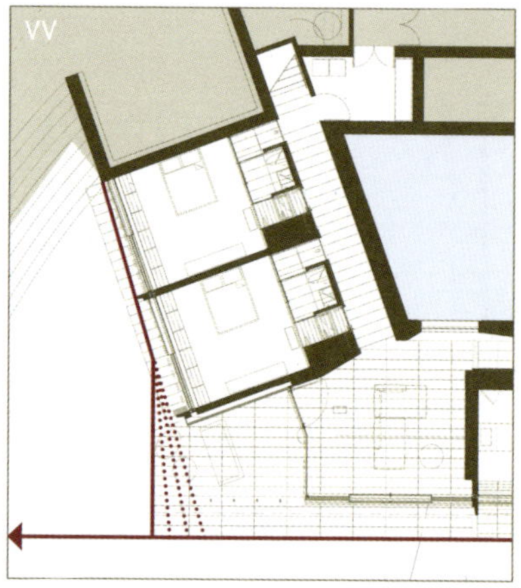

The plan of Villa Varoise conforms to a parallelogram, the result of deformation and accommodations of site conditions. Thus, while its layout might be characterized as a classic courtyard, its particular geometric disposition draws from the optimization of key views, zoning set-backs, and the standardization of repetitive parts. The lower level living area is set up as an exception to the standard parts, as two orthogonal geometries come into collision in the southeast corner. The porch canopy registers this collision by absorbing the eastern geometry and deviating from the southern face, giving the porch added protection from the sun.

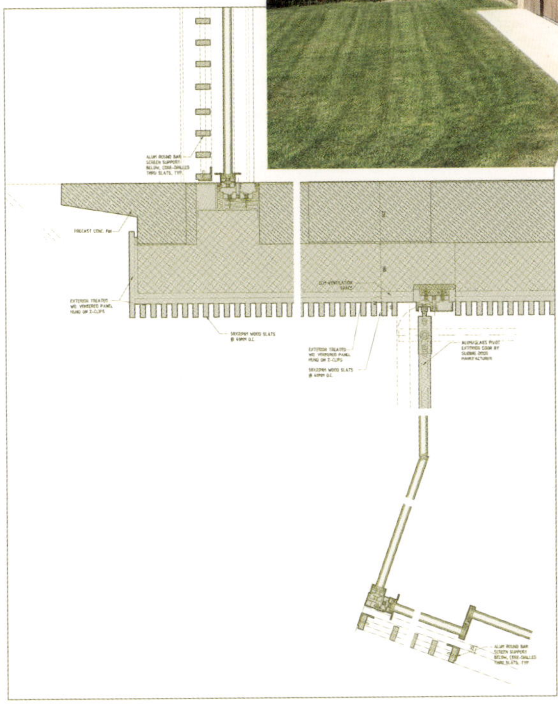
ALUM ROUND BAR
SCREEN SUPPORT
BELOW, CORE-DRILLED
THRU SLATS, TYP.
EXTERIOR TREATED
WD. VENEERED PANEL
HUNG ON Z-CLIPS
WOOD SLATS
VENTILATION
SPACE
EXTERIOR TREATED
WD. VENEERED PANEL
HUNG ON Z-CLIPS
WOOD SLATS
ALUM/GLASS PIVOT
EXTERIOR DOOR BY
MANUFACTURER
ALUM ROUND BAR
SCREEN SUPPORT
BELOW, CORE-DRILLED
THRU SLATS, TYP.

FH

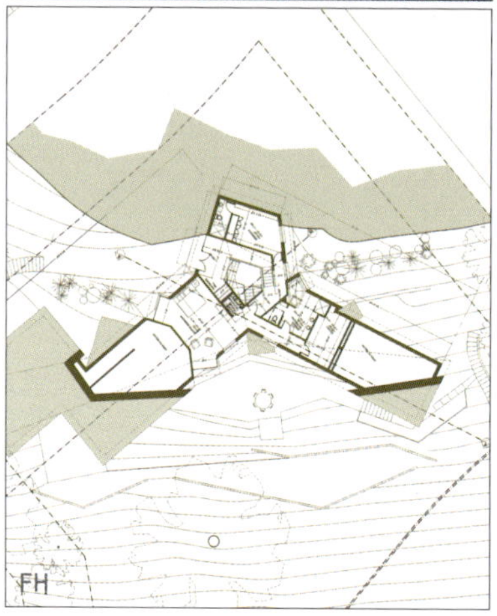

FH

these frontal windows is perpendicular to you. The opposite window, in the top floor, gives full bodied symmetry to that bedroom. The lower ones don't run into interesting problems, so they are just like everything else that isn't running into any trouble. There's a lot of the house that is just going on and doing what it does and the only thing interesting about it is that it's embedded in a giant parallelogram, one or the other wing of a bar that's bent in plan. A lot of details are kind of negligible and uninteresting. Now and then, there's a moment when you recognize a crisis, like that corner.

IR: Now I think there's one moment in the plan where the push out is in front of the staircase, which is the hinge of the entire thing that pushes out; there, it's effective. Then, when you push out in these other places, it all seems stylized.

PSC: That's so that the dining room can look out. I shouldn't resort to such things. Any number of students of mine would say "oh, you know, the dining's looking out there, and look what happens upstairs." I know it's lame to say that, but, let's look upstairs and this bedroom has it too, looking straight out and that is very nice if you're in this bed and there's another one looking oppositely toward the entrance so that you can see who is arriving to the house. They're symmetrically opposite each other. Look at that. I mean there is something interesting about what they do in the plan. All of this leads to your question: why bay windows? Bay windows are good things in houses, most people like them.

NT: All of these discussions bring up the question of abstraction, Scott. Because you're curating conventions, you're curating products.

PSC: I don't care about abstractions that much in this house.

NT: You don't care about it, but inevitably because you're so invested in all these little detail discussions about it, you are invested in certain ideas.

PSC: In hiding and seeking, both.

NT: In what?

PSC: Hiding and seeking it.

NT: Hiding and seeking what?

PSC: The abstraction. Hiding it behind the mask of something that looks completely conventional. Peter?

Audience [PETER ROSE]: I understand Tel Aviv, the Torus House and your own house in a continuum or as being part of a consistent body of

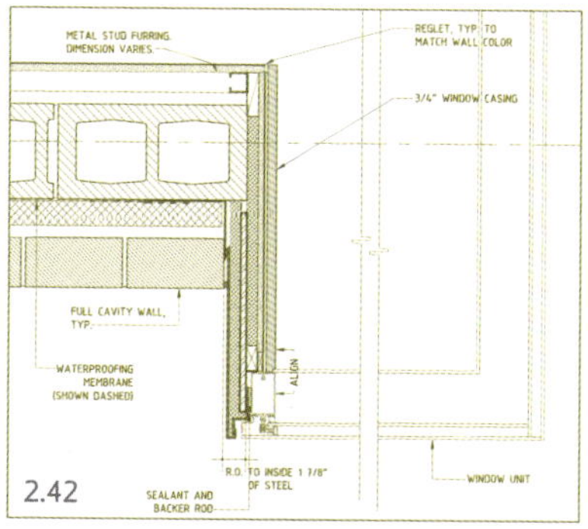

2.42

2.43

2.44

NT: Villa Varoise does not have fenestration in the strict sense: we do not punch windows out as such. The openings are merely the "space between" structural party walls. Sliding doors and brise-soleil allow for a seamless connection between the interiors and exteriors. In contrast, the fenestration of the Rock Creek House—for the same clients—display an attitude similar to the Fahmy House, as variable sized windows are strategically deployed on the southern face mirroring the organization of the interior. So too, the relationship between brick and glazing is used to test out varied programmatic opportunities in the space of the fenestration: on occasion flushing out on the exterior to develop inglenooks on the interior, and other times carving into the depth of the brick to display the masonry structure upholding the building.

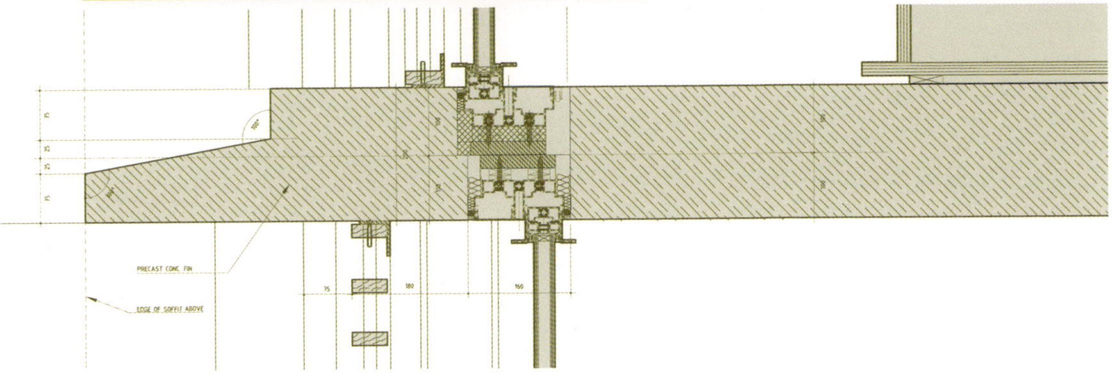
PRECAST CONC FIN
EDGE OF SOFFIT ABOVE
75
180
160

2.45

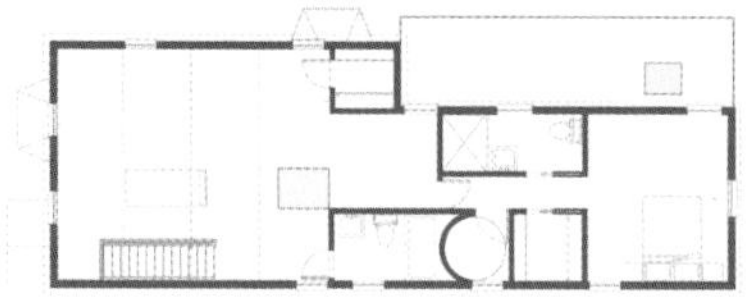

2.46

work. The exterior of your own house is kind of a given, you're trying to not make too much of a disturbance in the neighborhood, but the inside is extremely controlled, beautiful, precise, all of those things. Nader pointed out a change of personality or of motivation I think in, say this house which you defended in a bunch of ways. One was that the client wouldn't accept something, I think you said. What I'm interested in, is that this house, which is very interesting and is appealing on many levels, is a less powerful, more random work than I expect from you, and a less—the word aggressive is not what I mean, because I think your work is very graceful—but there's something casual about it, less disciplined even than—

PSC: Well what about that corner that I'm describing, how do you see it?

PR: I don't see it. You explained it, but most of the things you describe, I will see and then remember. But, I don't remember that one.

PSC: How about the fact that the whole house is a parallelogram? I mean you're not going to remember that? A gable form that is actually a linear building that's projected on the ground. Just that, nothing more.

PR: Maybe there's too much static, other stuff that gets in the way of—

NT: That's why I'm saying it's curated wrong. It's too much convenience.

PSC: If it hadn't been stone, would it be better? I can see that the fenestration and the projecting windows are distracting.

PR: But my question was why? What is it that's making you change? I think there's a kind of brilliance to the other.

PSC: The Torus House in upstate New York has discrete windows which give tautness to the membrane; the house in Cambridge, has several windows that are displaced to serve the spaces inside; the Tel Aviv Museum has windows caught between the geometry of the façade and the rooms inside. In the Goodman house and the Fahmy house, the windows look like the result of a lot of compositional motivation, though they are also related to particular conditions inside, as well. You might believe the windows are dedicated to rooms inside, but the conceit seems rather thin. It's pretty much like "oh, somebody's making a funky façade here, a strange façade, it's plastic, maybe even cast in place concrete," even though it's wood. I've had more than one person write me and ask me how we built a concrete house of this scale up on a hill in rural upstate New York. It's because of the abstrac-

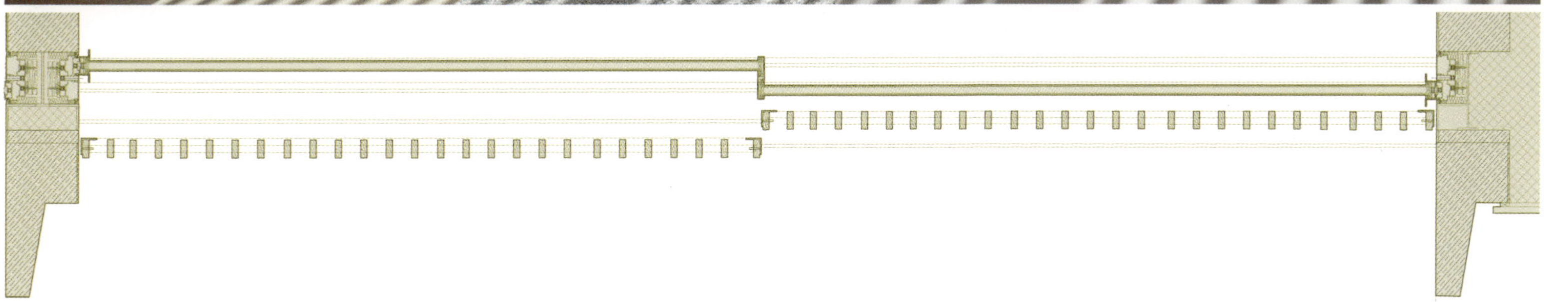

2.47

2.48

tion, the fact that these windows appear to be in disagreement with any kind of structural rationality. No one would punch windows like this, except in a cast in place wall. There's no framing that would be logical to support this, so it had to be a curtain wall, set off from the actual timber structure. It's almost like a commercial curtain wall cladding an old structure inside. In the Fahmy house, actually, the windows seem much more to respond to what is more ordinarily needed. I think its fenestration looks more purposeful; it looks more like the windows are dedicated to actual needs. They tumble with the building as it descends the hill, too. However, I don't think they're more willful here than in the other projects.

PR: I think the barn building has such a powerful typological sense to it that you can push it around and there's hundreds of years of buildings that have aberrant conditions that are the result of any number of factors. But, I think that this one doesn't have that—

PSC: Yes, the barn has that history and this is a new form.

PR: It doesn't have any overriding power that allows you to play this way. I mean, I like the work so much.

PSC: But I thought the rigidity of the parallelogram was pretty strong, considering the number of forms we could use today to make a house.

PR: So, what we would say to students, on occasion, would be that it may be stronger in your mind than it really is. I say that with great deference.

PSC: Maybe it's incorrectly rendered. If I had not used all these wrongful devices, could it be a strong enough form? A parallelogram that's bent, falling with the hill and that looks like a gable? That's my question.

Audience [CAMERON WU]: I think part of the problem is that the gable is in the wrong direction. I mean it's abstract because the gable is on that broad side and it gives us the image of this super wide very, very shallow gable, right? Which refers to the domestic, but is not oriented the proper way and so therefore I think it makes—

PSC: It's the back, so who's going to see it? That's a good point. But, if you do see it, it's a strong form for a contemporary house.

CW: But it's still abstract because you're claiming it refers to the domestic and the normal, but it doesn't because it's so mal-proportioned from the back. It's not a normal gable.

VV

In working with the local earth of the region, we found the concrete aggregate to be of a warm amber hue. The concrete serves as structural walls between bedrooms, with a raw finish. The openings in the bedrooms contain four layers of treatment: a translucent curtain, a blackout shade, a sliding glass door, and a sliding wood brise-soleil. All these elements are dynamic and move according to temperature, sun orientation and desire.

PSC: *We've already seen this with the Low House by McKim Mead and White and on Venturi's house. We've had the long gable form which has moved away from the normally proportioned gable you're referring to. I still think you'd read the gable-ness of it.*

CW: From the back.

FH

2.49

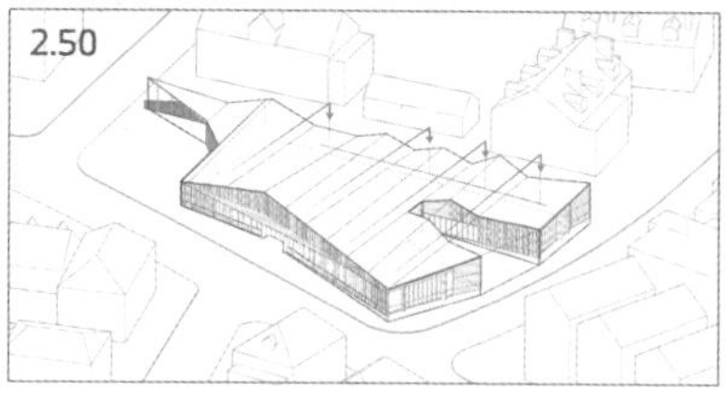

2.50

As an ongoing preoccupation since Casa la Roca we have been treating the roof as a fifth elevation: a tapestry that telegraphs the spatial logic of the interior. In the context of the Adams Branch Library the same logic helps to negotiate the civic and the domestic scales of the neighborhood.

PSC: *From up high in the back. No one could miss that it's a gable form...*

CW: Its very abstract. You're asking someone to float to see this house in elevation. Whereas the other view is very much about seeing it in perspective. From there the game is the—

PSC: *...that the gable is squashed.*

CW: The stone runs diagonally rather than horizontally.

PSC: *Ah, so the stone takes over, when it's seen from below. Whereas from the elevated view, seen from across the valley, the gable form is the stronger issue.*

Audience: Actually, I had a question. Because I came to know both of you through unbuilt house projects and specifically Torus house and Nader, your project with the big rock in the back and the brick wall, both from the 90s I would say? And I'm wondering about how those projects relate to your career over all, and where they situate themselves in relationship to the work you've shown today? To what degree do you think the houses we've seen today supersede or redefine a personal architectural project or act as a kind of continuum or refinement of those?

NT: Up till now, I've done eighty projects, but I don't present a majority of them. Casa la Roca is one of the unbuilt projects I still present and is central to my work. There is definitely a continuation. It is another one of those projects that was obsessively and overly controlled, but also, it's the curation of the brick and the block and the abstraction that is what keeps it in check. The only real misgivings I have about it are a result of a significant disagreement with my ex-partner who added more windows to the front and I was against those. Even then, I was already in the process of editing significant things out of the house if only to underline what I thought to be the key features to fight for. But for me that house was the beginning of a flirting with structural speculation, environmental speculation, and an idea about integration over which I had no knowledge but wanted to be invested in. Scott?

2.51

PSC: *I think that he answered how these projects continue. It just seems like one ongoing*

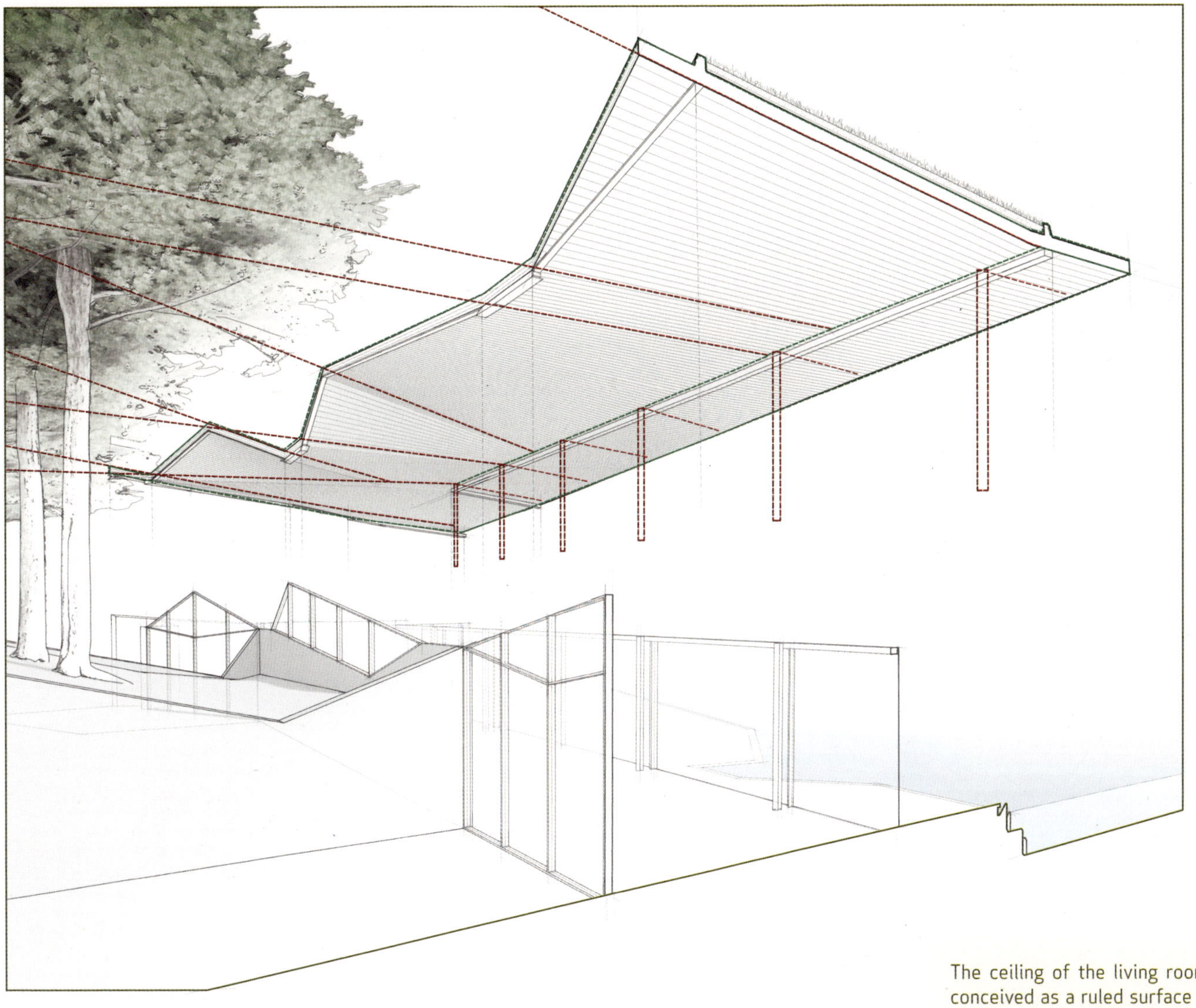

The ceiling of the living room was conceived as a ruled surface with a flat edge on the east, where the sliding doors open onto the courtyard; and a creased edge on the west, where clerestory windows reveal the majestic presence of the Pinus Pinea. This produces a structural asymmetry such that the east edge is supported by a row of slim steel columns, whereas the west is supported by a thick retaining wall that serves as a base for vaults overhead.

2.52

2.53

2.54

With economy in mind, the roof structure was ultimately triangulated to avoid the complex formwork associated with ruled surfaces. However, a view back towards the work of Louis Kahn, Sigurd Lewerentz, and Felix Candela sheds light on our original intent. The Candela canopy displays the geometric principle behind our original scheme. Kahn's Kimball Museum is famous for the development of roof figure that does not actually work as vaults spanning laterally, as would a Roman rendition, but rather longitudinally as would a beam. Curiously, the asymmetry of our structure, between the cadence of columns on one side and the folded vaults on the other, produces a hybrid structure, with longitudinal spans on the west, in tandem with lateral spans from west to east, connecting to repetitive columns. The effect of the interior view might be seen as similar to the longitudinal view of Lewerentz's ceiling in St. Mark's Church, with what appears to be random geometries, but what are in fact, pointed connections between concrete piers and steel columns.

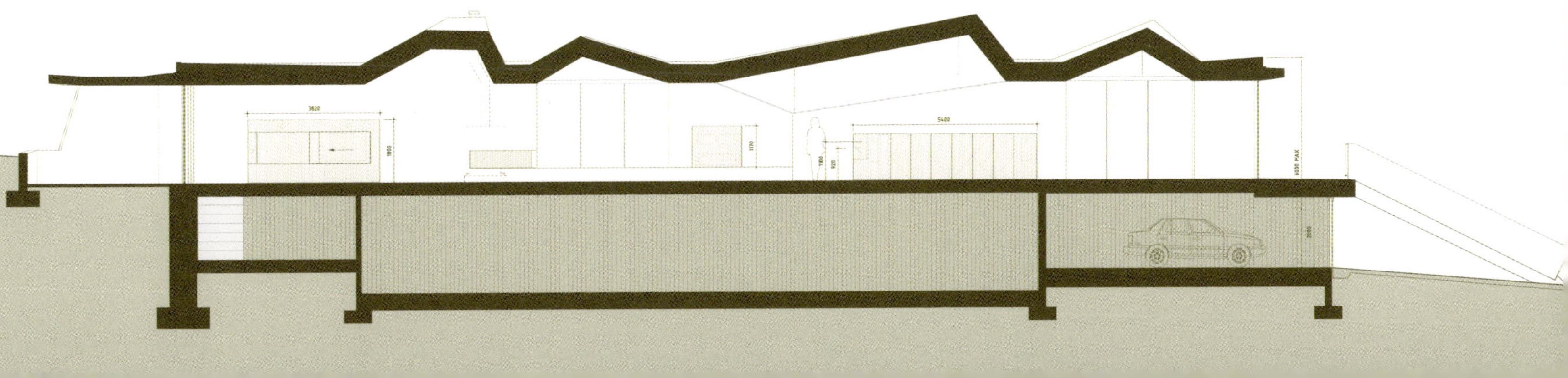
3820
1800
1170
1100
920
5400
6000 MAX
2000

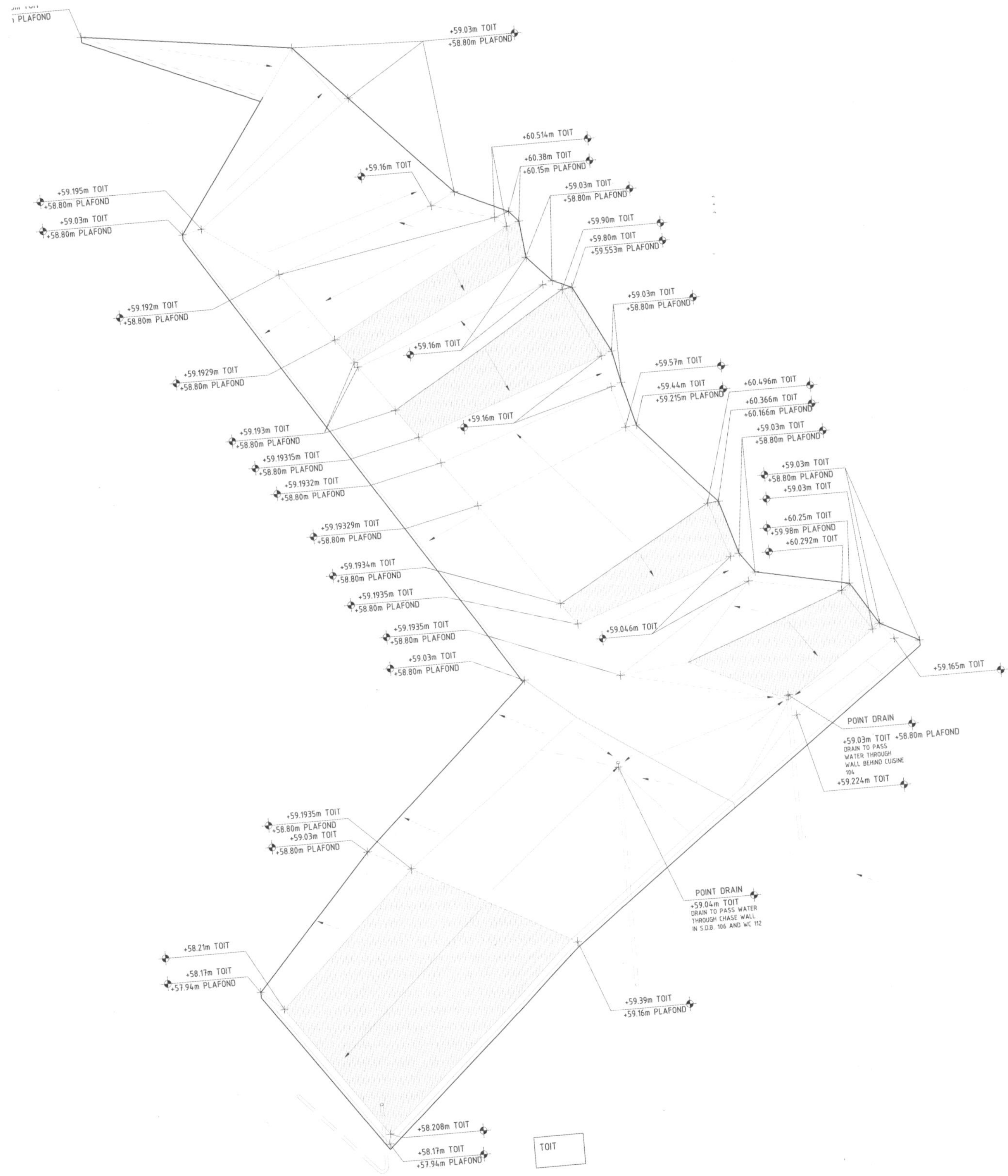

+59.03m TOIT
+58.80m PLAFOND
+60.514m TOIT
+60.38m TOIT
+60.15m PLAFOND
+59.16m TOIT
+59.195m TOIT
+58.80m PLAFOND
+59.03m TOIT
+58.80m PLAFOND
+59.90m TOIT
+59.80m TOIT
+59.553m PLAFOND
+59.192m TOIT
+58.80m PLAFOND
+59.1929m TOIT
+58.80m PLAFOND
+59.57m TOIT
+59.44m TOIT
+59.215m PLAFOND
+60.496m TOIT
+60.366m TOIT
+60.166m PLAFOND
+59.193m TOIT
+58.80m PLAFOND
+59.19315m TOIT
+58.80m PLAFOND
+59.1932m TOIT
+58.80m PLAFOND
+59.19329m TOIT
+58.80m PLAFOND
+59.1934m TOIT
+58.80m PLAFOND
+59.1935m TOIT
+58.80m PLAFOND
+60.25m TOIT
+59.98m PLAFOND
+60.292m TOIT
+59.046m TOIT
+59.165m TOIT
POINT DRAIN
+59.03m TOIT +58.80m PLAFOND
DRAIN TO PASS WATER THROUGH WALL BEHIND CUISINE 104
+59.224m TOIT
+59.04m TOIT
DRAIN TO PASS WATER THROUGH CHASE WALL IN S.D.B. 106 AND WC 112
+58.21m TOIT
+58.17m TOIT
+57.94m PLAFOND
+59.39m TOIT
+59.16m PLAFOND
+58.208m TOIT
TOIT

thing, to me. I don't see a break, really. One thing leads to another.

Audience [INGEBORG ROCKER]: But Nader, the attitude towards material seems to be changing because I think I'm seeing two different treatments in this building. One is extreme literal narrative, Scott was pointing out that the ingredients of concrete start to showcase their deliberation until they arrive at their primitive state of being rock, which I think is a narrative the previous projects seem not to have executed in this way. And then the other one is more from an interior use point of view where you show programmatically material associated to program bleeds into other spaces and therefore becomes hypothetical. What I'm talking about are the moments when you have the bathrooms and material of that penetrating outside of the bathroom into the hallway so you have these phasings of material encounters which essentially make no sense in a proper way, but evoke a presence of the pool's water body behind the wall.

NT: These are two different strategies.

IR: Yes, these are different items than what you, Nader, or what Scott is pointing out because the water and concrete are both one materiality which is teased or pushed to an extreme. On the one hand, we have the material extreme which extends from the logic of its behavior, and on the other, the overlay idea, which I think is a trace from encounters you had with Silvetti which is still more a question of the semantics of the window, the wall, the flattening of the chimney and all those kinds of things. So, it seems as if we have at least a shift here.

NT: But let's separate these two. First of all, to work in concrete, just on a fundamental level is very different than all of the other kinds of tectonic moves where you build up that way, aggregations. It's different. What I try to show in those two animations is that: A. You either work with aggregates in as an aggressive way as you would have in bricks or blocks and so that the dimension of the aggregates, the color of the aggregates, their material presence becomes evident in the formation of the house, which is the animation Scott showed. Or B. one falls into another tradition of "architecture parlante" where it's arbitrary, you can make any form out of it, which is kind of silly, but is obviously evident in the strain of our work. Why I like Casa la Roca is because, yes, the sidewall looks like a curtain, but it isn't a curtain, it is a laterally reinforced wall that brings in light and air in unprecedented ways and has a layered narrative to it. The way that I like the concrete house is that it is a direct

2.55

extension of that tradition. The bringing in of tiles and terracotta into a corridor is altogether different. It's a way of taking a servant space, a circulation space and, effectively, graphically animating it and, it's more of a Venturi kind of thing. It is not interesting at a material level. It is purely a graphic device. Now with that graphic device, something materializes in the wood of where you sit becoming the floor, or it becomes the furniture, it becomes programmatically laden. However, the idea of the tile coming in from the toilet and the other side is as graphic an argument as you can make and I think that's a separate issue. So, I like it less.

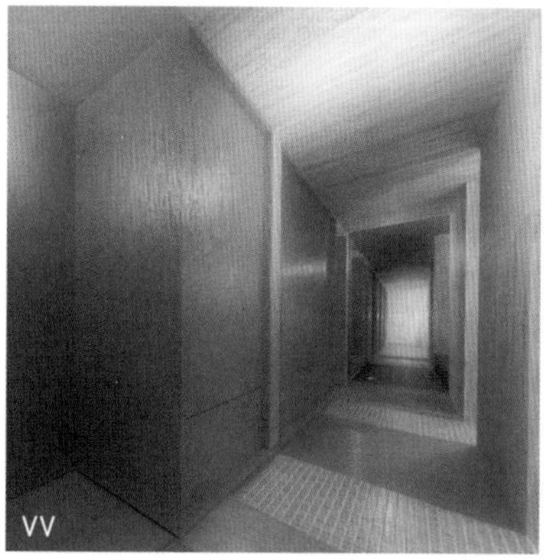

VV

PSC: I guess there are two very different kinds of transformative investments you're making. One is more typological, which I have a similar interest in, and the other is kind of this materialist redevelopment of the actual image of the building.

NT: But the typological was present in Casa La Roca also. And that was very much also a courtyard house.

2.56

PSC: But what's at stake in that material? The question I have is, what would happen if you didn't have the stone emerging from the concrete in that house? What if it was just a plain concrete wall or if it was just a plain brick or stone wall? Why isn't the typological investment sufficient for you?

NT: Because it's a rare instance where engineers speculate to transform the discipline of architecture. So, if we don't do it, we don't change the status quo. I feel the responsibility that we do need to motivate the discipline and produce not novelty, but innovation.

PSC: So you think that making the concrete gradient...?

NT: Absolutely.

PSC: ...to stone...

NT: Whether the argument is about optimization.

PSC: It's an innovation of ornament, in a way.

NT: Not only that. You may look at these things from a very different ideological point of view. Yes, you can...

PSC: But that's not the reason you're doing it. I mean you can use that alibi, but I don't believe it. I believe...

NT: Why don't you...

PSC: ...you take pleasure in seeing it go from smooth to rough.

NT: Why, am I not allowed...?

PSC: The gradient is not optimizing.

NT: Why am I not allowed to operate simultaneously as engineer, as architect, and as iconographer? Why can you not collude these different platforms?

PSC: On the other hand, you don't agree with Loos. You don't actually believe that many of these industries and technological developments—for example windows, mechanical systems, fixtures, hardware and whatever they may be—are part of a larger tendency, beyond our control. For you, it has to be taken under the single wing of the architect who artfully manipulates. One of the things that's a little bit off about the house-as-a-work-of-art, which is what I would say yours is, is that it's not about that larger problematic production of all those things. You will just do one little twist of it, but it's not having an effect on the totality of the system. The only thing you can manipulate, as an architect, it seems to me, are the inherent contours of the conventions with which we—

NT: I think we live in such a fragile discipline that we have to fight on every front from the doorknob to the house, to the public building...

PSC: Who are you fighting? What do you mean by that?

NT: We have a marginal presence in the world and...

PSC: So, you think architects have to take over the tasks of designing from other disciplines.

NT: Absolutely.

PSC: That will lead to the expansion of architectural agency?

NT: No, I feel we're very vulnerable and if we are speaking to ourselves, only like this, and not engaging in the industry, in different media and in different ways of engaging the world, essentially, we are only speaking to ourselves. Even if it was more symbolic, all of those years, even while I was here at the GSD, I was trying to suggest that we are also going to be engineers even though you know I was only making my little models.

PSC: I don't know what you mean by this, speaking only to ourselves versus speaking to the system. Architectural spaces and forms speak to their inhabitants or remain quiet in the background of their lives. Either way, our buildings are not only speaking to us, the architects. I also think the systems producers are ahead of us because they have already made everything

VV

2.57

2.58

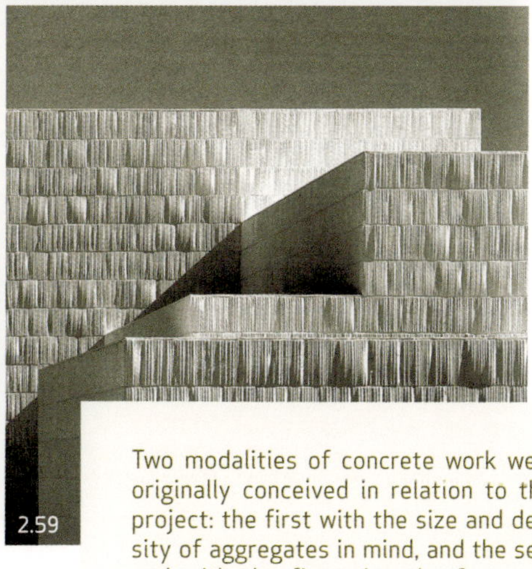

2.59

Two modalities of concrete work were originally conceived in relation to this project: the first with the size and density of aggregates in mind, and the second with the figuration the formwork might produce. Working with CNC milled high density foam, we developed mock-ups of rusticated walls, giving body to the depth of the concrete thickness. Other renditions also worked with fabric-formed frames that extended the rich traditions already experimented on by such figures like Andrew Kudless, Mark West, and Miguel Fisac.

custom to order within certain parameters so complex and very…

NT: Yes, and when you get into how they did it, you realize, "Oh, they're also doing it arbitrarily." So, we can contribute to it and change some parameters or we can change some material composition, and you prove through their system that you can use less material and say, "Oh, I like that better!" And the Macallen Building was one of those instances. We showed how we could lighten the structure, build it in less time, and have more flexibility in the layout. That's material and that's typological all at the same time. And it was the structure that preceded the organization of the entire building. That's real estate also, given its mission as a speculative project.

PSC: But you're combining arguments of optimization and technical refinement with your own ornamental and artistic gradient transformations, animated…

NT: I'm not blind to the conceits. Let's put it that way. I think we can erase a lot of instances.

PSC: It seems to me, actually, that if you were not allowed to make your physiognomic forms, you wouldn't be able to carry on this dialogue with the construction industry. You'd be robbed of the very agency or the very motivation to interfere with the industry. You wouldn't redesign the doorknob because there would be no reason to. What would you do? Just according to your taste, make a better, slightly rounder knob? I don't know why you would do that. It's only because you want the knob to be part of your neo-Art Nouveau language that it needs to be reshaped.

NT: No, the doorknobs are four different lines and they're not all Art Nouveau. Some of them do exactly what you're saying, they're totally conventional.

PSC: New standard types.

NT: No, they're very standard.

PSC: Then what do they contribute to the industry if they're not a new standard?

NT: They better the handicap hardware you get out there, for other reasons.

PSC: You don't think anyone in the world of industrial design can design a better knob?

NT: Sometimes not.

PSC: Only architects can do that?

NT: [Nod]

2.60

2.61

NT: For the Rural House, the board and batten system offers a tectonic mechanism through which the door handle may be encrypted into the logic of the cladding—which was essential for the anonymity of this façade. A conventional door knob would become too conspicuous on this occasion.

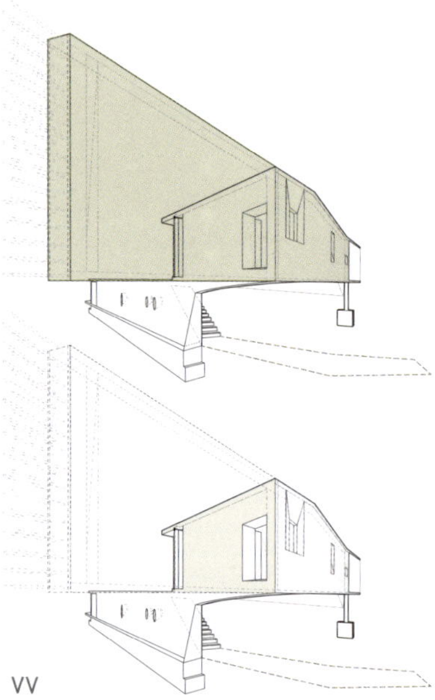

VV

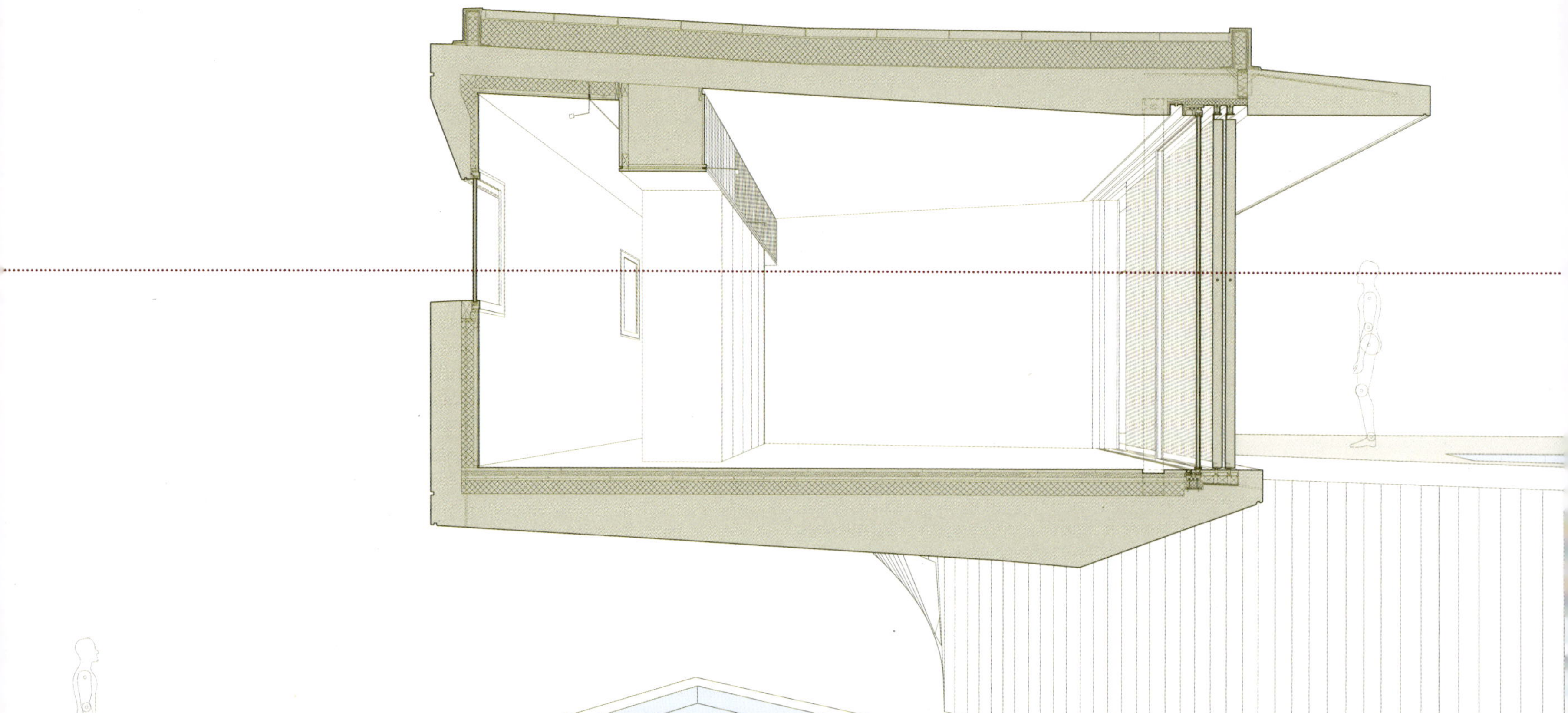

PSC: Ok.

NT: No, no that's not true. I mean there are people who are excellent furniture designers, but I'm saying it's possible that...

PSC: That an architect can do it better.

NT: Yes.

PSC: Well of course. And they could also do architecture better.

NT: And we've done lots of bad architecture.

Audience: Hi, thank you for coming here. I'm interested to know in conceiving each project at the concept level, what do you care about most or what do you think about first? Maybe in just one sentence.

NT: The production of new forms of knowledge. [laughter]

Audience: Could you elaborate?

PSC: Oh, I don't know. I don't have a single sentence like that. Actually, at one point when we had our previous conversation, I asked Nader a question like that. I asked what was at stake.

NT: It's a very ambitious thing to say. When you hear, "This is your ambition," you realize how little you're contributing to the discipline. Sometimes you contribute only this much and sometimes not at all, but I mean, when you see something great, isn't it amazing. Don't you get excited when somebody's done something great?

PSC: I guess I want to extend the repertoire of forms and types of buildings just a little bit. A little bit beyond what I inherited. That's as much as I can do. I don't want to compete with the technicians of other domains. I want to do that within architecture. I don't think the design of the doorknob is fundamentally an extension of architecture. This is a difference between us, and differentiates me from a lot of people. I think focusing on those domains is not uninteresting entirely and I agree that you could do it well or better than some of those who do it. However, I want to do it within what I consider to be the more fundamental spatial and social givens of building programs. I want to have that be the domain of innovation.

Audience [Ghazal Abbassy]: The domestic program is not for this kind of investigation? Why not?

PSC: I was talking about this with Sam, my thesis student, who is developing a very interesting public building that combines different kinds of spiritual spaces. This involves many

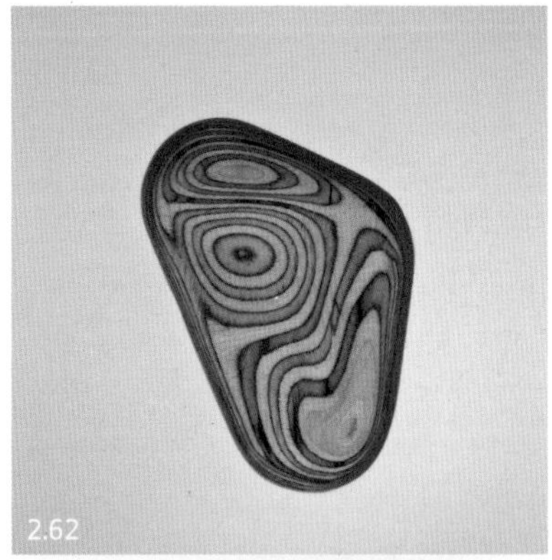

2.62

2.63

Rock Creek House, NADAAA

institutional and cultural practices. On the other hand, there are many systems, the kind that Nader masters so well and beautifully, which we didn't look at on the interiors of his bigger projects; the ceilings that absorb all the mechanical, lighting, and acoustical systems in a lot of interesting ways in the structure. I think houses have less complex systems, less cumbersome and difficult conditions and are not as obliged to present a decorous solution of the systems. You could have a kind of simpler, raw, and direct kind of experience in a house. Now, you can up the ante and try to make it all very refined. I think I prefer the house to be a more casual space, actually. But if we do things like fillet, the way Koolhaas did, in that building. What's the name of it?

NT: Educatorium.

PSC: Yes, Educatorium. Philip Johnson made the greatest statement of all, in defining architecture as "the art of wasting space." And, I thought, ok, you can absorb that kind of space that's useless in a public building because that actually relieves people of being confined to a norm which is so unrelentingly practical. Imagine if our second skin, our envelopes that are outside of our bodies denied us any pleasures or qualities of spaces to look at and to imagine ourselves moving in and they're just right up against us, flat at times and kind of like cages. I do think public buildings can relieve that by deploying wastefulness as the Educatorium does. I wonder, in a house, how often can you give up 30% of a space to produce the fillet? I mean all of the fillets that all of us love are kind of consumers of space and I think a house is a different domain, and I don't think Nader wastes space inside his houses either. That's right, and he does all this tiny stuff, shrinks the fillet into the details and I just get rid of the whole fillet because I don't think it belongs in the details either.

Audience [MARIANA IBAÑEZ]: In the context of that claim, where do you think, for example, the Ordos House is?

PSC: I think the bottom of the house is very public. A number of us did these huge houses, they were 10,000 square feet. My first question, at that first conference with the client was, "could we please reduce the house?" I wanted to make the house 3,000 square feet, not 10,000, and he said "the lowest I'll let you go is 9,000." So, I divided the house in two: a big sprawling entertainment villa and a private area for the actual people who live in this house. I made it almost like a museum with a house on top.

MI: No, but what I mean...

2.64

2.65

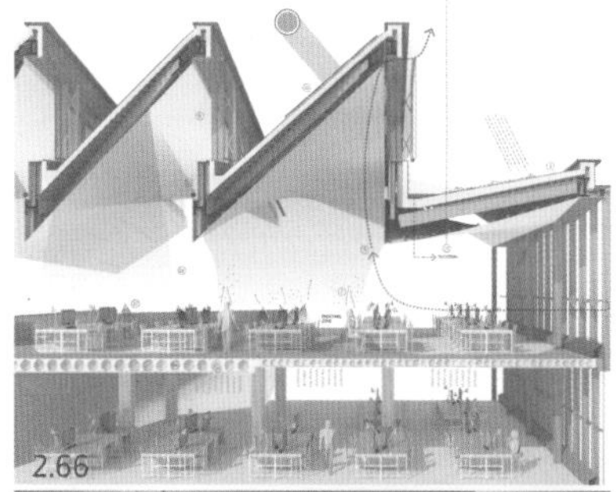
2.66

2.67

NT: This is an interesting acknowledgment, because it effectively communicates an attitude I was trying to communicate about Villa Varoise... and how the front façade takes on a more civic presence, almost like a museum if you will, but it still allows the massing of the head to be seamlessly connected to the figure of the entire body, the bedrooms, living areas, and all the other areas which have a more domestic character.

2.68

Ordos House, Preston Scott Cohen

PSC: This is just a house.

MI: I know, but because of the claim that domestic space lacks the formal opportunities, I'm interested in understanding the typological references…

PSC: It's an urban myth.

MI: Let's just say someday you do get a client that wants a 10,000-square-foot house where, if you take those same references and you distort them to that size they become actually…

PSC: I know, I actually wrote in that text that the problem with big, contemporary houses of architects is that they have become museums.

NT: It's funny that…

PSC: I think there's something vulgar, gigantic, and bloated…

NT: Loos's houses produce that public funding in the most institutional, monumental, and architectural way despite the argument you made.

PSC: Well, we may argue that they should present a public face.

NT: No, you did argue that, but…

PSC: To the city, and they do in a very restrained way…

NT: But, they're not like conventional buildings. They're highly estranged, sort of defamiliarized and they're—

PSC: But they're a new form of anonymity against the old which cannot exist in the classic world. Loos said we must develop a new suit to present ourselves in public space. Not a suit that's adorned with the past.

NT: New suit [pointing at audience member]. New suit. Here.

PSC: No, it has to be anonymous and restrained.

NT: Trust me, the Villa Varoise is very anonymous.

PSC: It is?

NT: Oh, absolutely.

PSC: Good.

NT: Stealth.

PSC: He likes the stealth. But when we get up close we can see that granular invention.

NT: It's part of the patronage.

Audience [CAMERON WU]: I think Nader felt guilty about jumping into the purer plasticity,

and felt the need to have some expression in the aggregation.

PSC: Actually, I think this question is more for you, Nader, than for me because I don't need to be innovative at the microscale.

NT: Well listen, I presented it with a sense of humility and guilt.

Audience: You've made a lot of references to Loos's plans. I was wondering, if he was here now, would he be concerned about the use of modernistic standard windows? Or would he be asking whether the core aspiration should be to go out of your way to spend a lot of human labor, energy, and material in order to maintain the landscape form as the current expression of indulgence? His critique of ornament was that it was indulgent on the eve of industrialized society. Is your desire to maintain the line of the landscape comparably indulgent?

PSC: You're saying the house expresses its excesses in all of the ways it tries to preserve the landscape?

Audience: Yeah. Is that the equivalent of what Loos—

PSC: Archi-ecological project?

Audience: Yeah.

PSC: It tries to and goes to an extreme to do so. This indulgence is meant to relieve the client's guilt for having harmed the environment, or something like that?

Audience: Yeah.

PSC: Bad faith.

Audience: Because it's the waste of human labor that Loos is interested in.

PSC: That would be a great critique to launch against many of the ecological, green architects.

Audience: Didn't you say, "the best dressed man is the one you don't notice."

PSC: Yeah.

Audience: So, it takes so much work and effort to make it unnoticeable. That's an argument.

PSC: It takes a lot of labor to make it unnoticeable. I don't know if this house...does it look so laborious to you? It isn't with so many precious details. What looks so labored about it?

Audience: You're asking me?

PSC: Yes.

Orange Tree
Fig Tree
Olive Tree
Vineyard
Sedum
Poppies

Lavender
Cyprus Tree
Oak Tree
Eucalyptus Tree
Pine Tree

Audience: I suppose, the simplest and most efficient thing to do would be to create a platform as people have done through convention and build a house on that platform to make a mark in the landscape.

PSC: I'm not sure, in this case, because of the topography I had to work with. We did a number of designs and this one very much minimizes the amount of cutting. We have the maximum allowable cut and fill. This is pretty tight.

NT: But you know what, the biggest critique—

PSC: You could look at it another way, but it would be the same. It's just the roof would step, but then you wouldn't get as much space inside. And, just having the roof be one big slope is not a very laborious solution.

NT: That's not it—

PSC: We have less edging, and less—

NT: The single decision to have used stone in Los Gatos where everything else is plaster is the most—

PSC: Stone is often used there.

NT: Really?

PSC: Yeah.

NT: Because they were very, very wealthy?

PSC: No, it's all cladding. All fake.

2.69

Audience: What is the structure?

PSC: Stone veneer on concrete construction. The cladding is very simple. It's very "all-American." It's nothing. It's not an exceptionally expensive house. You've got a big advantage over me in terms of your budget here, friend. Sorry.

NT: It's true.

PSC: You'd admit that.

NT: That's true. Have we had enough?

PSC: I think so. We've been at this for an hour and a half. We've had enough. Thank you so much.

NT: Thank you.

[Audience claps]

VV

VV

VV

3.1

3.2

3.3

3.4

POSTSCRIPT: THE WEIGHT OF PREDICAMENT

NADER TEHRANI

Drawing on themes from Harry Cobb's book *Words and Works, Scenes From a Life in Architecture: 1948-2018*, the presence of "predicament" looms large in this project, rooted in the inevitable conundrum that architecture is at once committed to a dual ethic: on the one hand, its usefulness to its inhabitants and on the other, its commitment to disciplinary advancement. It is a practice that is fraught at the outset, because the interests of these parallel ethics do not always easily coalesce. In the context of this project, that same predicament is amplified by zoning and board approval protocols that not only set rules on set-backs and massing, but also establish dictates on questions of character, materiality, and iconography. Compounding that, the patronage of residences involves a distinct temporal dynamic in which a "house, conceived as a piece of architecture" transforms into a "home, as a domestic setting"; this process of taking ownership does not necessarily happen when construction is complete, but rather is an extended temporal line that threads through the collaborative process of a commission. Beyond notions of ownership, *gemutlich*, and personal taste, this relationship also involves an emotional transposition that occurs when the client thinks that they are becoming the architect themselves. In part, Preston Scott Cohen's reference to the tensions between Loos and *Gesamtkunstwerk* speaks to this very issue, even if he does not touch on the psychopathological traumas shared between clients and architects.

This project then, even if initially drawn with academic poise, and subsequently advanced with meticulous interdisciplinary care still falls prey to a challenging process whose material vestiges become evident on the body of the building. Cast in the local earthen concrete, the stark regional materiality of Villa Varoise was premised on a dialogue with such mediations. Yet, impositions from the local municipality and equally predictable sentimentalities from the patron converged around the need for the familiar: stone walls, red tile roofs, wooden beams, and other such tropes that did not so much emerge from the core of a design process, nor an initial list of desires, but rather as impending confirmations of deeply-felt conceptions of home.

If this tension between disciplinary commitments and client desires hints at the architect's admission of weakness, or at least a caveat an architect would like to provide as alibi for deviations from disciplinary agendas, it is also not a defense. Since out of these experiences one recognizes that architecture, when all goes well, is the consummation of a near-perfect conjunction of representation and construction; but, it is also the recognition that when all goes wrong, there remains an important history of architecture that was never built, or even possibly meant to be built. Myths are made of those unbuilt projects. Alas, we now live in a moment when the space of architectural projection, in all its rendered realism, can come into conversation with the built evidence of its compromises after the fact, all of which can be refashioned, perfected, and reconciled through air-brushed effects in the post-production of architectural documentation. In comedies, the film commonly ends with bloopers, demonstrating the fecundity of the serendipitous in the process of making. Here, the comic is not so much felt in the moment of construction, but possibly in hindsight, when the editorial hand of representation comes to rescue the importance of architectural projection, as an idea. More than the rescue itself, the efforts to do away with error, with capitulations to clients, or with circumstances, guide us back to the value wrought by all these seeming externalities on what we have tried to control in our disciplinary zeal.

ACKNOWLEDGMENTS

I would like to begin by thanking the entire team at NADAAA for their continued contributions, energy, and the discipline they bring to our collaborative work. There are many individuals, and all bring something different to the table, but I do want to give special thanks to Arthur Chang, Richard Lee, and Harry Lowd for their many years of collaboration, patience, and authorship. Alongside them, Amin Tadj and Gretchen Neeley have had the same impact, but the bond of our friendship, going back many years, adds to this dimension of gratitude. Many people contributed to Villa Varoise, but Harry Lowd and Lisa LaCharité served as patient partners in the trenches, and the trips to Europe together added to the pleasure. Nicole Sakr meticulously and lovingly designed this book and were it not for her steadfast focus, we would never have gotten to the goal post.

As part of our extended team, I want to thank Shirin Raissi, whose discipline should be credited in the deployment of all construction aspects of this building. She served not only to translate words but a culture of design. Her own work and authorship precede this house, and her exemplary work on the interiors demonstrates the meticulous care she brings to her projects. By extension, I want to thank MAURO's construction team for the craft they brought to the entire project.

Katherine Faulkner served as my partner for the decade it took to design and build this house; she did so with immense professionalism, poise, and friendship, holding us all together in challenging times. During this same period, we have had the support of the Harvard Graduate School of Design, MIT School of Architecture and the Irwin S. Chanin School of Architecture. Each of them forms an important role in upholding the discourses that make for a book such as this. As part of this academic context, I want to thank Preston Scott Cohen in particular for the invitation to speak at the GSD, and further to that, to work diligently on this book alongside me. Robert Levit of the Daniels Faculty was also central in situating this work within a larger debate, as always with his razor-sharp insight and wit.

Beyond this, I would like to offer an immense thanks to the clients, who have asked to remain anonymous. They opened their life to us, their family, and the intricacies that define them as people. They are repeat clients, and this means they have also exposed themselves to the repeat offenses and pleasures of architecture; this rarely happens, and there is no substitute for this kind of support!

Nader Tehrani

PROJECT CREDITS

ARCHITECT
NADAAA
Principal: Nader Tehrani
Project Managers: Harry Lowd & Lisa LaCharité
Project Team: Rawan Alsane, Tom Beresford, Craig Chapple, Katie Faulkner, Dan Gallagher, John Houser, Ellee Lee, Kevin Lee, Parke MacDowell, Ryan Murphy, Jonathan Palazzolo, Joana Rafael, Caitlin Scott, Tim Wong

ARCHITECTE ASSOCIÉ AND INTERIORS
BIDARD & RAISSI (Paris, France)
Principals: Shirin Raissi & Marie-Eve Bidard
Project Manager: Majed Katir
Project team: Xavier Arrighi, Elsa Calcavino, Noam Carmi, Dani Haz, Jennifer Kandel, Eugénie Pellissier

CONSULTANTS
Mechanical Engineer: TPFI
Structural Engineer: ECI (Nice, France), Simpson, Gumpertz & Heger
Electrical Engineer: TPFI
General Contractor: MAURO
Landscape Architect: JEAN MUS
Lighting Designer: INEDIT
Furniture Consultants: CORSO EUROPA (Milan, Italy)
Home automation (Music & Cinema) : LIVEWIRE (UK)
Garden: ATRIUM & ARHAMI

PHOTOGRAHPY
John Horner Photography

ILLUSTRATION CREDITS

VV All drawings of Villa Varoise are copyrighted to NADAAA and all photography of Villa Varoise is copyrighted to John Horner Photography.

FH All drawings and renderings of the Fahmy House are copyrighted to Preston Scott Cohen, Inc.

1 THE ARBITRARY IS ARCHITECTURE

1.1 Office dA (1995). Casa la Roca. [Photograph of physical model]. Caracas, Venezuela.

1.2 Office dA (1997). Weston House. [Photograph of physical model]. Weston, Massachusetts.

1.3 Office dA (2003). Tongxian Art Center. [Photograph of physical model]. Beijing, China.

1.4 Grimshaw, John and Pauline (1999). The Minaret of the Friday Mosque 1110 CE. [Digital photograph]. Saveh, Iran.

1.5 Stroup, Neil (2011). Thomas Hockley House, Frank Furness. [Digital photograph]. Philadelphia, PA.

1.6 Office dA (1998). Toledo House. [Photograph of physical model]. Bilbao, Spain.

1.7 Tehrani, Nader (2018). Cristo Obrero Church, Eladio Dieste. [Digital photograph]. Estación Atlántida, Uruguay.

1.8 Preston Scott Cohen, Inc. (1998-1999). Torus House. [Rendering]. Old Chatham, NY.

1.9 Bildarchiv Preußischer Kulturbesitz (1927). The Weissenhof Settlement. [Postcard]. Stuttgart, Germany.

1.10 Tehrani, Nader (2016). Unite d'habitation formed concrete pilotis. Le Corbusier, 1952. [Digital Photograph]. Marseilles, France.

1.11 Horner, John (2018). Beaver Country Day Research + Design Center, NADAAA. [Digital photograph]. Newton, MA.

1.12 Concrete facade (n.d.). Edificio IBM building, Miguel Fisac, 1966-1967. [Photograph]. Madrid, Spain.

1.13 Horner, John (2009). Macallen Building, Office dA. [Digital photograph]. Boston, MA.

2 MY HOUSE IS BETTER THAN YOUR HOUSE

2.1 Office dA (1994). Mill Road House. [Digital photograph]. Madison, AL.

2.2 Harvard Graduate School of Design (2012). Preston Scott Cohen and Nader Tehrani. [Digital photograph]. Cambridge, MA.

2.3 Preston Scott Cohen, Inc. (1991-1992). Cornered House. [Rendering]. Sarasota, FL.

2.4 Preston Scott Cohen, Inc. (1991-1992). Cornered House. [Drawing]. Sarasota, FL.

2.5 Preston Scott Cohen, Inc. (1998-1999). Torus House. [Drawing]. Old Chatham, NY.

2.6 Preston Scott Cohen, Inc. (1998-1999). Torus House. [Rendering]. Old Chatham, NY.

2.7 Ocitim (2006). Kentucky Knob House, Frank Lloyd Wright. [Digital photograph]. Dunbar, PA.

2.8 Richters, Christian. Dutch House, OMA. [Digital photograph]. Holten, Netherlands. Courtesy of Office for Metropolitan Architecture (OMA). Rotterdam, The Netherlands. www.oma.com

2.9 Preston Scott Cohen, Inc. (2011). Tel Aviv Museum of Art. [Rendering]. Tel Aviv, Israel.

2.10 Preston Scott Cohen, Inc. (2011). Tel Aviv Museum of Art. [Rendering]. Tel Aviv, Israel.

2.11 Geron, Amit. Preston Scott Cohen, Inc. (2011). Tel Aviv Museum of Art. [Digital photograph]. Tel Aviv, Israel.

2.12 Sambonaris, Victoria. Preston Scott Cohen, Inc. (2004). Goodman House. [Digital photograph]. Pine Plains, NY.

2.13 SHoP Architects. Museum of Sex (1998) - and - FIT New Academic Building (2010). New York, NY.

2.14 Preston Scott Cohen, Inc. (2010). Taiyuan Museum of Art. [Digital photograph]. Shanxi Sheng, China.

2.15 Berger, Albert and Imagno/Getty Images (n.d.). Ornament and Crime, poster by Adolf Loos for a lecture on February 21, 1913. [Colour lithograph]. Österreichischer Ingenieur-und Architektenverein.

2.16 Office dA (2003). Rural House. [Digital collage]. New England.

2.17 Preston Scott Cohen, Inc. (1998-1999). Torus House. [Drawing]. Old Chatham, NY.

2.18 Villa Snellman exterior photo (n.d.). Gunnar Asplund, 1918. [Digital photograph]. Djursholm, Stockholm, Sweden.

2.19 Brown, Timothy (2004). Muuratsalo Experimental House, Alvar Aalto. [Digital photograph].Muuratsalo, Finland.

2.20 L, Seb (2016). Stahl House, Pierre Koenig. [Digital photograph]. Los Angeles, CA.

2.21 Ramblersen (2014). House of Finn Juhl. Finn Juhl, 1942 [Digital photograph]. Charlottenlund, Denmark.

2.22 Preston Scott Cohen, Inc. (2010). Taiyuan Museum of Art. [Digital photograph]. Shanxi Sheng, China.

2.23 Preston Scott Cohen, Inc. (2010). Taiyuan Museum of Art. [Digital photograph]. Shanxi Sheng, China.

2.24 Preston Scott Cohen, Inc. (1998-1999). Torus House. [Rendering]. Old Chatham, NY. http://www.prestonscottcohen.com/project13.html

2.25 1985 Chevrolet El Camino (n.d.). [Digital photograph].

2.26 OMA (1998). Y2K House. [Photograph of physical model]. Rotterdam, Netherlands. Copyright Office for Metropolitan Architecture (OMA). Rotterdam, The Netherlands. www.oma.com.

2.27 Preston Scott Cohen, Inc. (2008). Inman House. [Digital photograph]. Cambridge, MA.

2.28 Preston Scott Cohen, Inc. (2008). Inman House. [Digital photograph]. Cambridge, MA.

2.29 House of the Silver Wedding in Pompeii (n.d.). Atrium and the peristyle, c. 300 BC. [Digital photograph]. Pompei NA, Italy.

2.30 Mary Miss (1977-1978). PERIMETERS/PAVILIONS/DECOYS. [Digital photograph]. Nassau County Museum, Roslyn, NY.

2.31 Tadao Ando Architect & Associates (1981-1998). Rokko Housing Project I, II, and III. [Drawing]. Kobe, Japan.

2.32 Horner, John (2003). Rural House, Office dA. [Digital photograph]. New England.

2.33 Burt Reynolds in 1970s (n.d.). [Poster].

2.34 Comb-over (n.d.). [Digital photograph].

2.35 Jeffrey Mayer Photography (2010). Justin Bieber at Variety's 4th Annual Power of Youth Event.

2.36 Heintz, Paul, Local Studio (2017). Concrete at Taliesin West, Frank Lloyd Wright. [Digital photograph]. Scottsdale, AZ.

2.37 Motion Array (n.d.). Water Pouring into Glass. [Digital photograph].

2.38 Freepik, Kues (2016). Concrete Wall. [Digital photograph].

2.39 RECKLI GmBH (n.d.). 1/21 B Malta concrete, Vertically arranged elevations with mid-coarse chipped patterns, separated by approx. 15-millimeter wide depressions. [Digital photograph].

2.40 Atelier Peter Zumthor (1996). Therme Vals interior. [Digital photograph]. Vals, Switzerland.

2.41 Garner, Kurt. Brick worker's cottage, late 1800s (2009). [Digital photograph]. Indiana Dunes National Park. Lakeshore, IN.

2.42 NADAAA (2016). Rock Creek House, NADAAA. [Drawing]. Washington, DC.

2.43 Horner, John (2016). Rock Creek House, NADAAA. [Digital photograph]. Washington, DC.

2.44 Horner, John (2016). Rock Creek House, NADAAA. [Digital photograph]. Washington, DC.

2.45 Preston Scott Cohen, Inc. (2008). Inman House. [Digital photograph]. Cambridge, MA.

2.46 Preston Scott Cohen, Inc. (2008). Inman House. [Drawing]. Cambridge, MA.

2.47 Koch, Raimund. Preston Scott Cohen, Inc. (2004). Goodman House. [Digital photograph]. Pine Plains, NY.

2.48 Sambonaris, Victoria. Preston Scott Cohen, Inc. (2004). Goodman House. [Digital photograph]. Pine Plains, NY.

2.49 NADAAA (2019). Adams Branch Library. [Rendering]. Dorchester, MA.

2.50 NADAAA (2019). Adams Branch Library. [Drawing]. Dorchester, MA.

2.51 Office dA (1995). Casa la Roca. [Photograph of physical model]. Caracas, Venezuela.

2.52 Stvan, Jeff, FOR[A] Photography (2011). Ceiling Detail, Kimbell Art Museum, Louis I. Kahn. [Digital photograph]. Fort Worth, TX.

2.53 Torra Pla., Josep Maria (2009). Ceiling detail, St Mark's Church, Sigurd Lewerentz. [Digital photograph]. Björkhagen, Stockholm, Sweden.

2.54 Candela, Antonio and Erwin Lang (n.d.). Entrance to Lederle Laboratories, Felix Candela and Alejandro Prieto, 1956. [Photograph]. Mexico City, Mexico. Progressive architecture, 9/1/1957, ISSN: 0033-0752, Volume 38, Issue 9, p. 144.

2.55 Office dA (1995). Casa la Roca. [Photograph of physical model]. Caracas, Venezuela.

2.56 Office dA (1995). Casa la Roca. [Drawing]. Caracas, Venezuela.

2.57 Matsys (2009). P_Wall (2009), San Francisco Museum of Modern Art.

2.58 BCHO Architects with Mark West and C.A.S.T. University of Manitoba (2009). Hanil Visitors Center & Guest House. [Digital photograph]. Danyang-Gun, South Korea.

2.59 Centro cultural Castilblanco de los Arroyos facade detail (n.d). Miguel Fisac. [Photograph]. Castilblanco de los Arroyos, Spain.

2.60 Office dA (2009). Macallen Building, NADAAA. [Drawing]. Boston, MA.

2.61 Horner, John (2003). Rural House, Office dA. [Digital photograph]. New England.

2.62 Horner, John (2016). Rock Creek House, NADAAA. [Digital photograph]. Washington, DC.

2.63 Horner, John (2016). Rock Creek House, NADAAA. [Digital photograph]. Washington, DC.

2.64 Haefner, James. Preston Scott Cohen, Inc. (2017). University of Michigan, Taubman College of Architecture and Urban Planning. [Digital photograph]. Ann Arbor, MI.

2.65 Werlemann, Hans. Educatorium, University of Utrecht. OMA. [Digital photograph]. Utrecht, Netherlands. Courtesy Office for Metropolitan Architecture (OMA). Rotterdam, The Netherlands. www.oma.com

2.66 NADAAA (2018). Daniels Building at One Spadina Crescent, University of Toronto, Daniels Faculty of Architecture, Landscape, and Design. [Drawing]. Toronto, ON.

2.67 Lehoux, Nic (2018). Daniels Building at One Spadina Crescent, University of Toronto, Daniels Faculty of Architecture, Landscape, and Design, NADAAA. [Digital photograph]. Toronto, ON.

2.68 Preston Scott Cohen, Inc. (2007-2008). Ordos House. [Photograph of physical model]. Dongsheng District, Ordos, China.

2.69 DK Images, Pinus Pinea Illustration (n.d.).

3 POSTSCRIPT: THE WEIGHT OF PREDICAMENT

3.1 En bateau (2010). Vue de Ramatuelle. [Digital photograph]. Ramatuelle, France.

3.2 Rodriguez, Santos Martin (2011). Cáceres Arco de la Estrella. [Digital photograph]. Cáceres, Spain.

3.3 Stocksy (2015). Detail of Old Stucco Painting on Wall. [Digital photograph]. Provence, France.

3.4 Plain arrow loop, Aughnanure Castle Heritage Site (2015). [Digital photograph]. Oughterard, County Galway, Ireland.

ORO EDITIONS

Publishers of Architecture, Art, and Design
Gordon Goff: Publisher
www.oroeditions.com
info@oroeditions.com

Published by ORO Editions

Editor: Nader Tehrani
Book Designer / Editor: Nicole Sakr
Text: Nader Tehrani, Preston Scott Cohen, Robert Levitt
Drawings: Harry Lowd, Lisa LaCharité, Gary Lin
Transcription: Nathan Vice, Tofan Rafati, Nicole Sakr
Photography: John Horner
Font: Apex Sans by Chester & Rick Valicenti
ORO Project Coordinators: Kirby Anderson, Jake Anderson

10 9 8 7 6 5 4 3 2 1 First Edition
Library of Congress data available upon request. World Rights: Available
ISBN: 978-1-951541-34-7
Color Separations and Printing: ORO Group Ltd.
Printed in China.

International Distribution: www.oroeditions.com/distribution

ORO Editions makes a continuous effort to minimize the overall carbon footprint of its publications. As part of this goal, ORO Editions, in association with Global ReLeaf, arranges to plant trees to replace those used in the manufacturing of the paper produced for its books. Global ReLeaf is an international campaign run by American Forests, one of the world's oldest nonprofit conservation organizations. Global ReLeaf is American Forests' education and action program that helps individuals, organizations, agencies, and corporations improve the local and global environment by planting and caring for trees.